DC Police Stories 1

DC Police Stories 1
Text Copyright © 2017 by LT Marco F. Kittrell MPDW

All rights reserved. No part of this book may be reproduced or transmitted in any form or by any means, electronic or mechanical, including photocopying, recording, or by any information storage and retrieval system, without written permission from the publisher. The only exception is brief quotations for reviews.

The character's names have been changed, but the events are true.

For information address:
J2B Publishing LLC
4251 Columbia Park Road
Pomfret, MD 20675
www.J2BLLC.com
GladToDoIt@gmail.com

Printed and bound in the United States of America.
This book is set in Garamond. Designed by Mary Barrows.

ISBN: 978-1-948747-08-0 Paperback
       978-1-948747-09-7 Hardcover

DC Police Stories 1

LT Marco F. Kittrell, MPDC retired

The Dedication

This book is dedicated to the memory of all the police officers who lost their lives serving their country and respective police departments.

For without their dedicated service and devotion to your beliefs, so many would have suffered. To those officers and their families, we salute you and may God bestow his blessings on your families.

        LT Marco F. Kittrell, MPDC, (ret)

Acknowledgements

Where do I start? I have been in law enforcement for over 45 years. I started at the age of 17 years as a police cadet. I was so young and ready to start my career, after a little encouragement from my mother.

I was sitting on the couch eating a jelly sandwich and watching cartoons on the television; wearing a pair of shorts and a white t-shirt with holes all through the shirt. I had just graduated from high school a month earlier.

My mother walks by carrying a clothes basket filled with clothes that she had just finish washing. Mom stops in front of the television set. She looks at me, places the basket down on the floor, and asks me what my plans were now that I have completed High School.

I told my mother that I wasn't sure, and I would find something after the summer. My mother walks over to me, bends over, looks me right in the face and says, "Marco. That police department down town is trying to locate some young men for the police department. What do you think?" I told my mother that I would check into it the next day. My mother, being the way she was, responded, "What the hell is wrong with right now?"

That was when I knew it was time to get moving. My mom gave me the look that only mothers give their children when they want you to do something … no matter how old you are.

I was on the police force for the next 25 years because my mother motivated me. I owe her a lot. She was very close and involved with my children and grandchildren.

My mother died in 2002, and I miss her so much; even today. I wish I had more time with her because she was so important to my family. But, I am so glad that my children knew their grandmother.

My father was also important to me in that he was a very big part of my life; always there when I needed him. I thank him for that.

My wife Dorothy motivated me to write this book. Without her inspiration and constant drive to better this project, I don't believe I would have completed this manuscript. To her I owe everything in finishing this book. She was the one who stayed on me, reviewed my work, and corrected it, when necessary. My wife's love and belief in me was the driving force that helped me to finish and publish something that is very important to us; a summary of my life as a young man who matured into a policeman. I love her and thank her for that support system that I so much needed.

I would like to thank Mrs. G. Delores Ellerbe, Mrs. Lillie Thompson Martin, and Mr. Alton Roundtree for their support and dedicated service in helping me with this project. I'm in your debt. Thank you for your kindness and inspiration.

Table of Contents

Introduction   1

Police Cadet

1. Officer Clarence Thomas 1972   5
2. The Jail Riot 1972   13
3. My True Love 1974   21
4. Officer Mark Johnson 1974   29

Police Officer

5. Mr. Ted Williams 1975   37
6. Officer Walter Pope 1975   41
7. My First Homicide Case 1975   49
8. Ms. Smith 1975   55
9. The Great Dog Chase 1975   59
10. The Great Safe Robbery 1975   67
11. The Jungle 1975   71
12. Cadillac Jim 1975   79
13. The Parking Lot 1976   95
14. The Man That Change My Life 1976   99
15. My Best Friend 1976   109
16. The Constructive Worker 1976   115
17. My First Suicide Case 1976   121
18. The Traffic Accident 1976   129
19. A Man in Love 1977   135
20. Mr. Johnson 1977   143
21. Detective John Smith 1977   149

22.	The Little People 1977	159
23.	Mary 1977	167
24.	South Capitol & Southern Avenue 1977	173
25.	Officer Mark Shawn 1978	177
26.	My First Police Shooting 1978	183
27.	Out On My Own 1978	189
28.	My Sister 1978	195
29.	The Unusual Burglary Suspect 1979	199
30.	Trying to Make a Living 1979	203
31.	The House Fire 1979	209
32.	My Second Police Shooting 1980	213
33.	The Dentist Office 1980	221

Sergeant

34.	The Young Major 1981	229
35.	A Lady 1981	239
36.	My Girl 1982	247
37.	The Little Girl 1982	253
38.	Sergeant James Frank 1983	267

Lieutenant

39.	The Arm Robbery Gone Bad 1992	275
40.	Officer James Brooks 1992	279
41.	Officer Helen Books 1993	293
42.	The Chase 1994	303
43.	Can You Help a Friend? 1994	309
44.	We Are All Gone 1994	317

My Retirement Celebration

45.	The Red Sports Car 1975	323
46.	Sergeant Walter Johnson 1975	331
47.	The Full Moon 1976	337
48.	Tex 1982	341
49.	**The Wall 1982**	347
50.	My Children and Grandchildren	351
51.	Too Many Police Funerals 1995	353

Introduction

I started my police career on Monday, June 2, 1972, as a Metropolitan Police Cadet in Washington, DC. That is a program that hires young men and women between the ages of 17 to 19 years old and prepares them to become police officers in the great city of Washington, DC.

I really had no idea what to expect from the department. I was young and somewhat inexperienced in the way of life. I had no idea what lay before me as a police cadet or as a police officer. However, I learned very quickly what is needed to be a police officer in Washington, DC.

For three years, I worked in only two division assignments; Community Relations Division and Traffic Division. They both were great jobs. I met a lot of important people and had a great time working there. I performed mostly public relations work for the department. A few months before I was scheduled to attend the Police Academy, I was transferred to the Traffic Division.

I used every possible contact that I had to have the transfer canceled, but to no avail. Everyone told me that it was to my benefit to get some exposure to real police work. I didn't want to hear that. I wanted to keep my good inside job in community relations.

Thanks to others who cared for my benefit, I was transferred to the Traffic Division. It turned out to be one of the best assignments I ever experienced. I met new friends and learned a great deal about police work that benefited me later as a police officer and supervisor. These are the reasons why young people need to experience new things, places, and take on new adventures.

Once I completed and graduated from the police academy, I was assigned to the First District Sub Station located on Capitol Hill. I work there for one year. I requested a transfer to the Seventh District located in the South East sector of the city. I worked there for 5 years and really learned how to become a police officer. Later my experiences there made me a better police supervisor and manager.

I was promoted to Sergeant in 1980 and was assigned to the Fourth District, located on Peabody Street, Northwest. I worked as a patrol sergeant and later as an administrative sergeant for the police district.

In 1983, I was promoted to Lieutenant and reassigned back to the Seventh District. I was a Sector Commander and supervised/managed four sergeants and 33 police officers.

During my 12 years as a lieutenant, I was the commander of:

- Vice/Task Force that targeted and investigated illegal drug criminal activities and prostitution offenses.

- Detective Investigation Section that investigated all criminal activities.
- Investigation Unit called Rope that targeted career criminals and repeat offenders.

This book covers some of my experiences while working as a policeman from 1972 to 1995.

I hope everyone who reads this book will appreciate the sacrifices that police officers make every day to keep citizens and their families safe. To you we say, "Thanks for your dedicated service."

I have changed the names of all parties mentioned in the book. Even though the stories are true, I wanted to protect the families, especially the children, of the police officers. These stories in no way are geared to disrespect my fellow police officers or their families.

I simply would like to share my experiences with you and others; especially young police officers. As a young man I made several mistakes as an officer, but learned from them to better myself and became the police manager that I am today. Most leaders are not born into the job. They learn from their mistakes and turn those incidents into successes for others to benefit from.

I had the pleasure to socialize with many good police officers; men and women. They helped me and assisted with my growth, not only as a policeman but as a man as well.

Police Cadet 1972 to 1975

Officer Clarence Thomas 1972

Chapter 1

I was seventeen years old and a police cadet working at the Seventh District, Metropolitan Police Department (MPDC) located on Mississippi Avenue in Southeast, Washington, DC. The Seventh District had just moved there from Chicago Avenue. I was very young, but I wanted to be a police officer. In the District of Columbia, you had to be twenty years old to be a police office. I just had to wait three years. I had time.

My first assignment was to work in the police station as a police clerk assistant. I really enjoyed that job. All the police officers would give me a hard time, but I know that it was all in fun. It was like a rite of passage for the young guys.

Officer Clarence Thomas always talked to me. He told me to hang in there and not give those officers any attention. He was teaching me how to become a police officer. He was my first true friend on the police force. Officer Thomas was only 25 years old and was like a big brother to me.

Officer Thomas was married with three children. He had a very pretty wife and was a lucky man. I couldn't understand why he dated so many other women. I guess it was the thing to do in those days. All the police officers did it and talked about it.

Sometimes, those officers would get off at 11:00 p.m. and go to the clubs, parties, or some woman's house. This always seemed to me not the way to live.

I wanted something better. But, I did learn a lot of things by talking with those officers when it came down to being a police officer. They would tell me a better way to handle myself when confronted with certain decisions, but Officer Thomas was always the best. He really talked to me and wanted me to learn the proper way of handling myself as a police officer.

One morning, I arrived at work at approximately 5:30 a.m., and I saw Officer Thomas walking out the back door of the police district.

He said, "Hi Kittrell, I'm going to handle this last assignment."

It was to assist a woman who wanted to leave her husband, but she wanted to take some clothes from their apartment. We on the police department called these assignments, Clothes Runs. Officer Thomas was working the midnight tour, 11:00 p.m. to 7:00 a.m. shift.

Approximately 10 minutes later I heard, over the police radio, Officer Campbell, Officer Thomas's partner, requesting an ambulance. Officer Thomas had been shot and was unconscious. Officer Campbell also stated that he had shot the suspect who shot Officer Thomas and the suspect was also unconscious. I couldn't believe my ears. I had just finished talking to Officer Thomas approximately 10 minutes earlier and now he had been shot.

The officers and supervisors immediately began exiting the police district as if the building was on fire. When an officer is shot, everyone goes to help. I wanted to go also, but as a police cadet I wasn't allowed on such crime scenes. That is just how it was.

I frantically attempted to get information on the condition of Officer Thomas, but there wasn't any. It seemed like the world had stopped. There was very little conversation on the police radio except for the occasional request for additional police units to perform other duties concerning the incident, such as blocking off streets, canvassing the area for witness, and other administrative duties.

I asked the other police officers who were in the police station what did this all mean. The words that I heard shocked the hell out of me.

"Kittrell," they said, "most likely the officer has been killed."

I just refused to believe that you could be talking with a man one minute and the next minute he is dead. I had never experienced such an emotion before. I asked the officer, "How do you know such a thing?"

He said, "By the way the officers were talking on the radio, you could tell that the officer was dead. All the officers were talking real slow and had no sense of emergency in their voices."

The ambulance arrived and there was no more information. Approximately five minutes later, the officers on the scene advised that Officer Thomas was being transported to the hospital. Twenty minutes later it was confirmed that Officer Thomas had succumbed to his wounds. The suspect who had shot the officer was also dead.

I went to the bathroom and started crying. I didn't want the other officers to see me crying, because I felt they would think of me as being weak. I later learned that it was nothing wrong with a police officer crying. During my 45-years career, I cried many times for many reasons.

This was my first, but certainly not my last time.

When Officer Campbell came back to the police district, I asked him, "What happened?"

Officer Campbell told me that as Officer Thomas entered the apartment building, they were met by a lady, later identified as a Ms. Janice James. Ms. James wanted to leave her husband, but she wanted to take some clothes with her and her husband refused to let her take some items out the house. Mr.

James was confronted by the police officers. Officer Thomas convinced Mr. James to allow his wife to leave and take some clothes with her. Mr. James was very pleasant and there was no reason to think there was any problem to suspect. Officer Campbell was looking down at the floor the whole time telling me this story and talking very slowly.

"Once Ms. James retrieved her clothes, we escorted her out the apartment and started walking down the steps. They lived on the second floor. As we reached the front door, Mr. James walked down the stairs behind us.

"We didn't hear him as he approached. Mr. James yelled out, 'You aren't leaving me, you bitch!' and fired a double barrel shotgun at Officer Thomas, striking him in the stomach. I then fired three rounds at Mr. James, killing him instantly. I grabbed my partner, but he was already dead. It only took seconds.

"I don't know how we could have been so careless. You never turn your back on anyone until the assignment is over. That is the general rule. We were both tired and let our guards down. How could we be so stupid? Just wasn't thinking, just not thinking."

Even in death, Officer Thomas was still teaching me.

Never turn your back, until the assignment is over; never! This was the first time I had known someone who had been killed, and I was having a hard time dealing with it.

Approximately one hour later, the commanding officer

was in the station talking to the officers, explaining what had just happed concerning Officer Thomas when Mrs. Thomas, Officer Thomas' wife, entered the police district. Her actions live with me today.

Mrs. Thomas slammed her hands on the front desk at the counter and said very loudly, "Keep the body, just give me the money."

I couldn't believe what I had just heard. The women just lost her husband. Her children's father is dead and the woman tells everyone, "Keep the body." What a bitch! The commander told Mrs. Thomas that they had been trying to reach her and asked if they can go to his office and talk about the matter.

Mrs. Thomas said, "Hell no! I know Clarence is dead and my children and I will be okay. Just pay up. I know the rules."

The room went dead with silence.

Officer Thomas and his wife did not have a happy marriage. Officer Thomas was running the streets and dating other women. I guess his wife didn't care about him anymore. Even so, I thought maybe Ms. Thomas could have acted the part of being a grieving widow. I never knew that a person could hate another human being in the way Mrs. Thomas hated her husband. For the sake of the children, I just believed that Mrs. Thomas would have played the role of a grieving widow. I guess not.

The Commander just said, "Mrs. Thomas, if you follow me I will explain the process to you."

During the funeral, Mrs. Thomas didn't cry at all. She kept looking at her watch as if to indicate that she was in a rush. Mrs. Thomas even attempted to flirt with another police officer at the funeral. I just said *that will never happen to me.*

I really missed Officer Thomas. He was like a big brother to me and treated me like a brother. In the short time that I knew him, I really knew what it meant to have a friend.

I never cried for a person in the way I cried that day. As I stated, it wouldn't be the last time I would cry while working as a policeman.

The Jail Riot 1972

Chapter 2

I was a police cadet working in the station administrative office. At approximately 8:30 a.m., the sergeant walked into the station and said that there has been a riot at the District of Columbia Jail House. Several correctional officers had been assaulted and taken prisoner. Three officers were even killed. Every police officer and cadet available was needed to quell the riot. The sergeant said, "Everybody get your shit together."

At seventeen, being a police cadet appeared to be very exciting, but the police officers working in the station were not so enthused about taking the assignment. I was very shocked to hear some of the comments that the officers made. Such as,

"Why do we need to go?"

"We are needed at the station."

"Our job is just as important as those guys working on the streets."

"We always get the short end of the stick."

I was very surprised and even embarrassed. Their comments made me feel as though they were acting like cowards and didn't want to leave the safety of their office to help other police officers.

Prior to this incident, I admired the officers assigned to the station, because they always had the right answers concerning the administrative aspects of the police department. They were good officers, but didn't like working on the street. They were very hard workers and dedicated, if they were working inside. They knew everything that was needed to address any issue that could arise concerning the running of the station. They kept everything going.

The sergeant looked at the officers as they were still complaining about their possible new assignment, laid his clip board on the table and said, "You sorry, lazy ingrates. People have been killed and maybe even more officers might be killed and all you can say is, 'you don't want to go.' I tell you what, every one of your sorry mother fuckers are going and will be the first officers on the entry team; you better believe that. Get your shit ready or give me your badge and gun and quit. We will find somebody to replace you sorry fuckers; any more comments?"

The room went quiet and the officers started looking at each other like no one knew what to say after those comments.

The sergeant yelled out, "Well, get moving and get your gear together and meet me in the rear of the station in 10 minutes. We have a bus that is going to take everyone to the jail. Now let's move like you have some balls attached to you."

Everyone started moving, including me. I liked the way the sergeant took control. The station is normally staffed with five officers. On that day, we had only two.

As the officers were attempting to locate their riot gear, it was the funniest thing I ever observed. I observed officers who hadn't worked on the street in years attempting to locate their riot equipment in their lockers; equipment that wasn't there. Every time an officer grabbed a piece of equipment, it either fell apart or it just wasn't there. I said to myself, I will never be like that.

The officers finally got themselves together and boarded the bus. The other officers on the bus that had been working on the streets for years started making fun of the station crew. Making comments like,

"I hope you boys aren't kidnapped by the inmates; they will have their way with you."

"When the firing starts, you officers will go in first, that way it will not be a great loss."

"Do you boys know how to use your firearms? That is that piece of metal you carry on your side. They call it a gun."

Everyone started laughing, but I could see that the officers assigned to the station were very concerned about being deployed to combat a riot at the jail.

Once we arrived at the jail it was crazy, but organized. Immediately as we exited the bus, the sergeant started getting the officers organized. Every officer from my police district was assigned as the second entry team. I could see that the police department was about to enter the jail and reclaim it. Officers were in formation with riot gear and armed with shotguns and gas launchers. It was about to get bloody. The supervisor and managers were giving directions; directions which resulted in the inmates being seriously hurt. In those days the philosophy was, "we against them; kick-ass and take names."

As a police officer cadet, I was not authorized to carry a firearm, nor could I make arrest, so I was given a traffic assignment. I wasn't happy with it but, I was going to do my part.

The police department attempted to negotiate with the inmates but the talks failed, and orders were given to prepare to retake the jail by any means necessary. I knew at that time several people were about to be seriously injured.

It was at that time that Congresswomen Shirley Chisholm arrived on the scene and asked if she could attempt to negotiate a settlement. The department agreed and a short time later the crisis was resolved. The inmates returned to their cells and the jail officers and police departments re-took the jail without the use of violence.

The injured and dead bodies were recovered.

The disturbance originated from the inmates complaining about the food that was being served to them daily. I learned then that it was the small things that could lead to bigger things, if you don't address them promptly. It is the appearance that you give to people and the way you respond to their concerns that is the key element to resolving police problems. People do not like being mistreated or dictated to as to indicate they don't have a say in their lives.

The inmates knew they were people who had been charged with crimes committed against the community and were waiting for their day in court. They still felt like they were human beings and wanted to be treated as such, regardless of their present situation.

Also, I learned later that inmates sometimes start riots to kill other inmates. Several inmates were killed and later investigation revealed that this was also the case. These suspects were identified, prosecuted, and convicted, as well as those inmates who killed the correctional officers.

I learned a lot that day, especially about myself and the officers with whom I worked. I didn't look down on the station crew because they were afraid of entering the jail. That wasn't the kind of police officers they were. Yes, they received the same pay and training, wore the same uniform, attended the same police academy, and took the same oath, indicating that they would serve and protect the citizens of Washington, DC. But, all police officers can't perform the same duties. Some officers are good at some things concerning police matters and not good at other police functions.

Working in the police station these officers were fantastic. Things got done and everything was processed according to plan. Working on the street wasn't their calling. I didn't like the way they acted during the emergency. As I progressed during my career with the police department, I learned that it took all kinds of men and women to get the job done and all police officers aren't suited for the same career path. Yes, we are all policemen, but travel different paths; some officers work on the streets and others in the station.

The jail riots made me respect the officers that were willing to enter the jail and put their lives on the line for others. Yes, some officers just wanted to break heads and kick ass, but other officers wanted to help and get the injured and hostages out before they were hurt further. I also learned a lot about the police department. We were well organized and able to address any given issue. Those qualities made me feel like I was part of something, a real professional organization. Yes, there were problems, but on that day the department looked, sounded, and acted like we knew what we were doing. I wanted to be part of the club.

I really admired Congresswomen Shirley Chisholm. The lady took control of the situation, put her own life in jeopardy, and saved many lives that day. I never felt she really received the recognition for her service to the community that day. There were some newspaper and television reporting of the incident, but you had to be there to see the congresswomen in action and how she handled herself during such a demanding time. It really was something to see. During those times women didn't receive the recognition and respect as their counterparts did.

A few years later Congresswomen Chisholm was the first female to run for the Office of the President of the United States. I voted for her. Congresswomen Chisholm died in 2005.

During my 45-year tenure in law enforcement, I was confronted with many demonstrations, riots, armed barricades, hostage takings, and other similar incidents. I always remembered 1972 as the year that prepared me to handle such situations and to conduct myself as a professional when confronted with so many variable circumstances.

I still worked with the officers that were assigned in the station. I just knew where I stood if I was confronted with such a situation again. When the officers retired, I attended their ceremonies. I always remembered the jail riot, when the Master of Ceremonies spoke on an officer's bravery during their career. I just smiled. They made it, working in the station during their tenure. What can you say?

My True love

1974

Chapter 3

"I am love and you are love, why do we not love"
LT Marco F. Kittrell, MPDC, (ret)

Sergeant Tommy Chase was a very good man and police supervisor. As a police officer cadet, I liked working with him. He always taught me things concerning police work. He was very patient and always eager to answer questions from me; a real pro.

The sergeant oversaw the police station, as we called it. All the prisoner processing and administrative work was performed in the station. It was a very busy place and an important one.

I loved working in the station. You could learn from the officers as they were processing prisoners and perform other tasks. I learned from the good officers and the bad ones. Sergeant Chase always told me, "Whatever you observed in the station, stayed in the station." This was our business and nobody else's. Everything went through the sergeant.

The sergeant took pride in his job and everyone, especially the police officers, respected him. On many occasions, things would happen from prisoners attempting suicide or escapes to injuries to police officers and prisoners. If Sergeant Chase was working; the lieutenant and captains never came to the station to investigate the incidents. They always said, "If Sergeant Chase is working, he was on top of the situation."

I love the respect that the sergeant was shown by everyone. I wanted to be like the sergeant.

One day during our shift and within an 8-hour tour, we had three different fights break out in the station, a prisoner attempted suicide, and a police officer had a heart attack in the station and died. The sergeant didn't miss a beat. Everything was handled like a well greased machine, by the book, and we got off on time. What a day! I loved working in the station. Something was always going on.

The sergeant always told me the right things when it came to police work. He knew all the when's, how's, who's, and what's. He had all the answers for the questions. The sergeant motivated me. I couldn't get enough of what he had to offer a young man who wanted to be a good police officer.

Sergeant Chase had one problem; women. The man could never keep a woman. I couldn't understand it. The sergeant had everything going for him: good looks, career, money in the bank, and no children. He was a real professional and he owned several properties all through the city. I just didn't get it.

The sergeant worked very hard at his profession and sometimes I wanted to tell him to slow down. But, who was I to tell him? I was a mere police cadet, a young man 19 years old. The sergeant had been policeman for 25 years and was 49 years old. The sergeant was older than my father. As time went on, the sergeant talked to me as if I was a friend and not a police cadet. That made me feel good, in that I was accepted by him. I thought because I was married and had two children, he looked at me differently.

Then it happened; a day that I will never forget. Officer Mary Scott was assigned to the Seventh District station and to our shift. Officer Scott had requested a transfer from the Sixth District and had just arrived.

It was reported through the grapevine, not official channels, that she was transferred because of her off-duty activities; dating too many married policemen that worked at the Sixth District.

A friend of mine who worked at the Sixth District called me and gave me the heads up.

He said, "Marco please watch-out for this officer. She had three different police officers leave their wives and after she had taken all their money, she left the police officers with no money."

This woman was so treacherous that she had two police officers buy her a house at the same time. How she pulled that off, I just couldn't imagine and didn't want to know. Officer Scott even sued a police officer for failing to marry her and won the case.

Officer Scott walked into the station and Sergeant Chase was hooked. The sergeant looks at her and he looked like the love arrow went right through him. I said to myself, *my friend is hooked like a fish on the line.*

Officer Scott was the most beautiful woman I had ever seen. She looked like a movie star. Her walk was like a queen entering her palace. It made every police officer and even the women look at her. One female police officer said, "Look at that bitch. Who the hell does she think she is, queen of the country?" I smiled and said to myself, *with those looks and walk, she could be.*

Because Sergeant Chase was her immediate supervisor, he took her into his office and gave her the good old welcome speech. The sergeant normally took approximately 15 minutes welcoming a new officer to the station. This time he took almost an hour.

The other officers working in the station started talking about the sergeant and making fun of him. I didn't like that. The officers made comments like,

"The sergeant must didn't get the memo about the other officers and their divorcés."

"I hope the sergeant isn't getting a table dance. I heard she was really good at that."

When Sergeant Chase and Officer Scott exited the office, I could tell the sergeant was hooked. For the next two weeks, the sergeant and Officer Scott worked very closely together on every issue. Officer Scott kept saying she couldn't do something and the sergeant addressed it like she was a little girl in need of some type of toy. It was a sad thing to see.

One month later, it was official. The sergeant and Officer Scott were dating and two months later she moved into his house. They kept that a secret, but you could tell.

The sergeant's conduct was totally not the norm and he acted like a little kid in a candy store. He couldn't get his fill of Officer Scott, like his glass was always empty.

Four months later, the sergeant announced that Officer Scott and he were engaged to be marred. This was the talk of the police department.

Many police officers that knew Sergeant Chase attempted to talk him out of the marriage, but his mind was made up. He knew what he was doing. The sergeant and I never discussed the marriage. I guess he felt, what could a 19 year-old tell him or he didn't want me to tell him my real feelings.

On several occasions, the sergeant would ask my opinion of Officer Scott as a police officer, but never their personnel life. Maybe this was his way of attempting to talk with me about Officer Scott and I was just too young to catch on. Sometimes later in my life, I regretted the opportunity that was offered and the fact that I never used it to talk freely with him.

I wanted the sergeant to be happy. Maybe we were all wrong concerning Officer Scott and maybe she wasn't the kind of person that most officers indicated. Prior to the wedding, all the officers started calling Officer Scott, "The Thing."

I already knew how police officers could be cruel, so I wasn't surprised to hear the comments. I really felt that most of the officers in the district liked and respected Sergeant Chase, but I was wrong. Most of the officers were just small minded and made fun of my friend.

It was a very big wedding. They got married at a five-star hotel with 500 invited guests. The sergeant even flew in a large portion of Officer Scott's family from Alabama and paid for their accommodations. They went to Hawaii for two weeks on their honeymoon. At the wedding, the sergeant looked so happy.

On their return, they both acted like they couldn't stay away from each other. Officer Scott was reassigned to the Youth Division and worked across the city from us. Approximately one year later, the problems started.

The sergeant wanted the marriage to work, in that he really loved her. They went to counseling, went on many vacations, and the sergeant gave her everything she asked for. But nothing appeared to work.

The sergeant was a different man. His performance at work was appalling and he was given a bad rating and reassigned to the midnight shift.

They finally got a sad divorce and my friend never recovered. His life just got worse. He sold all his properties as result of the agreement during the divorce.

The sergeant just couldn't take it anymore and he retired from the police department. He just came to work one day and submitted his letter to retire immediately. It was a sad thing to see, how a man could have such a great career and one day walk away as if nothing had happened the past 25 years. This really touched me and I said *I hope God gives me the strength to retire with my head up high and walk away.* I wanted to go on my own terms and not anyone else terms.

The sergeant and I stayed in touch with each other for the next 10 years. He came to all my promotions and personal celebrations in my life.

The sergeant died in 1986 of a heart attack. His sister found him in his house after being dead for a week. It was a very big funeral and I was very upset because of my friend's death. Officer Scott attended the funeral and we talked. She told me that she really loved Sergeant Chase and wanted to renew their marriage vows, but the sergeant refused.

She further told me that all the properties that were awarded to her as result of the divorce she returned to the sergeant a few years after their divorce. The sergeant never told me that and even to the present day, I wandered why. She further told me that the sergeant really cared for me and respected me as a man. I was so touched by the comments that I almost cried.

Officer Scott never remarried nor had children. She retired in 1990 and moved back to Alabama. Officer Scott died in 1995 of a heart attack. I hope they both found peace.

I really believe they both were looking for love and found it in each other, but at the wrong time in their lives. I wish they could have made it. Life is too short. Enjoy what you have. Don't let other people dictate your happiness.

Officer Michael Johnson
1974
Chapter 4

"A man chooses his own path, so why can I not choose mine"
LT Marco F. Kittrell, MPDC, (ret)

Officer Michael Johnson was only 24 years old when I first met him. He was a very good officer, but had many demons and hidden secrets. I was seventeen years old and had been a police cadet for three months. When I first met Officer Johnson, I was working in the police station filing police reports.

Officer Johnson approached me and asked if I was attending college while waiting to attend the police academy. He further stated that I should prepare myself in all ways to be successful as a police officer. We talked for about an hour and after the conversation I felt I had found a new friend. The officer also asked if I attended church regularly, because it helped police officers to better combat the daily stress of performing police duties. I was always attempting to broaden myself and

I had noticed that Officer Johnson was always attempting to motivate the young police cadets to attend college.

The next day, Officer Johnson reminded me to register for school and said, "Every day not in school was a day lost." I really felt that the officer was a good man attempting to motivate all the police cadets in doing well in their endeavors.

A week later, while working in the station, Officer Johnson arrested a man for beating the man's wife. As the officer was processing the prisoner, the officer, with his hands, struck the prisoner in the face for no apparent reason, causing the prisoner to fall to the floor. Officer Johnson stated the prisoner attempted to reach for his firearm, and he had to subdue him before the prisoner took his weapon.

The prisoner denied attempting to take the weapon and the officer had just hit him. I said to myself, *maybe I didn't see the entire incident and Officer Johnson was telling the truth.*

The other officers just laughed and said, "The prisoner deserved what happened to him."

Three days later as I was leaving for the day, I observed Officer Johnson removing a prisoner from a police cruiser in the back of the police station and throwing the prisoner down to the ground. Officer Johnson then grabbed the prisoner by his hand, as he was handcuffed, and dragged the prisoner into the police station. I said to myself *that was brutal and unnecessary.*

The next day I spoke with Officer Tom King, an officer

that I trusted, and asked him about Officer Johnson. I explained to the officer the things that I had observed and was troubled about Officer Johnson's conduct. I couldn't understand why a man who always talked about attending church and encouraging young people to attend college could be so brutal.

The officer told me something that I just didn't imagine about Officer Johnson. It seems that Officer Johnson was known for his aggressive behavior towards prisoners and citizens.

Every time the police department investigated allegations of abusive behavior against Officer Johnson, the charges never stuck. Officer Johnson always beat the charges. On two other occasions, I observed aggressive behavior on the part of Officer Johnson. The first was beating a prisoner who allegedly struck Officer Johnson and the second was a prisoner who fell down the stairs while exiting the police station in the officer's custody.

This was getting to be too many cases of abuse and I wanted to do something about the conduct. But, I was only a seventeen-year-old police cadet and no one would listen to me, especially policemen. It was a very special club and I wasn't part of the club, as a police cadet. But, the incidents bothered me very much.

I went back to Officer King and told him how I felt. It was making me feel very weird and I didn't want to be around Officer Johnson. I couldn't understand how the police department allowed an officer to be so brutal and not do anything about the incidents.

Officer King told me that the allegations concerning Officer Johnson would be addressed and to give it time. I felt the officer was just brushing me to the side because I was so young. I respected Officer King, but he did at times talk to me like I wasn't a member of the police force; like I couldn't be trusted and was not part of the group, an outsider.

A month later, as I was attempting to confront my feeling about Officer Johnson I learned that the officer had thrown a prisoner down some steps and the prisoner's arm was broken. The department initiated an investigation concerning the allegation of police-misconduct. I said, *finally maybe something will be accomplished.*

After the department's investigation, it was determined that Officer Johnson would be charged with several crimes against several different prisoners that he had assault over the past few months. I was sad, but relieved that something was finally going to take place. I couldn't see how a man could go on hurting people the way Officer Johnson was hurting people.

On the day that Officer Johnson was suspended, pending the outcome of the investigation, I observed him walking out the front door of the police station. He was smoking a cigarette and looking disturbed as if he had lost his best friend. I wanted to say something to him, but I didn't know what to say.

He looked at me, smiling saying, "Kittrell go to school and get that degree that you will need. Don't make my mistakes. See you in a few weeks."

I didn't say anything. I didn't know why. I just froze, thinking, *how can a man be so kind, but so brutal.*

I had seen several officers leave the police station after being suspended from duty and they all had the same look; as if their world had come apart and nothing was left to live for.

When a police officer is suspended, most policemen take the belief that they are no longer a man or women. They lose their gun, badge, police identification, and they lose their membership on the team. They are now an outsider, a nobody. All policemen get that look when suspended from duty. It is a sad look and Officer Johnson had the look.

The next day when I reported to work, I learned that Officer Jonson had committed suicide after leaving the police station. Like most policemen, he had another firearm at home. It was reported that the officer had a steak dinner, smoked a pack of cigarettes, called his mother, said that he loved her, and seconds after hanging the phone up, he placed a revolver in his mouth and blew his brains out.

This was the first time I was confronted with a suicide concerning a person I knew. It wouldn't be the last. I didn't cry. I felt sorry for a man who appeared to have everything going for him; youth, a proud profession, strong family ties, and a faith in God. Then I asked myself, *why a man does the things Officer Johnson did?*

When I attended the funeral, I believed I learned the reason why. I overheard some senior police officers who, had retired years earlier, who knew Officer Johnson's father who was also a police officer. Officer Johnson's father was killed in the line of duty by a prisoner whom he had arrested for arm robbery. Officer Johnson was only five years old at the time of his father's death.

I guess Officer Johnson held the world at fault for his father's death and wanted to take it out on every prisoner he arrested. That was such a sad way to live and go on with one's life. I never wanted to be like that and always told myself that I would always guard against blaming any one for my errors or loss.

Officer Johnson taught me one valuable lesson when I became a police officer. Be your own man and don't blame others for things that they had no part in. I wasn't going to live a sad and unproductive life as Officer Johnson.

I also blame the department for Officer Johnson's conduct. People knew, but did nothing. This sad story would stay with me for the next 45 years as a police officer.

If you see a wrong, correct that wrong before things get out of hand and someone gets hurt.

Police Officer
1975 to 1980

Mr. Ted Williams

1975

Chapter 5

"To love a person is to love one's self"
LT Marco F. Kittrell, MPDC, (ret)

Mr. Ted Williams was 93 years old and lived in the 100 block of Shipley Terrace, Southeast. He had been living there for 60 years. His wife died last year and he was missing her very much. They had been married for 73 years. Mr. Williams was a retired school principal.

I first met Mr. Williams a year earlier. I was walking the foot beat in his area and saw Mr. Williams drinking lemonade on his front porch.

He said, "Good morning Officer. Would you like something cold to drink on this fine hot day?" That was the beginning of our Friday morning breakfast club.

I used to stop by his house every Friday and eat pancakes

in the morning. Mr. Williams really enjoyed my company and me his companionship.

We used to talk about the worldly events and problems. Mr. Williams had visited many countries and done many things. He was my ideal of what a man should be when he reaches the age of 90 plus.

Mr. Williams home looked like a museum because of the beautiful pictures that his wife had collected. Every piece had a story and a special place in Mr. Williams' heart for his wife.

Mr. Williams always talked about his wife. If we talked for two hours, 90 percent of the time was about his wife.

On this day as we were sitting on his front porch drinking ice tea, Mr. Williams didn't look very well. He wasn't talking very much and it didn't appear that he wanted company. I asked if he was feeling well and that I could stop by later.

Mr. Williams said, "Please stay and let us talk a while."

Mr. Williams told me that he had a dream last night about his wife and she told him that he was coming home very soon. She said, "Don't be scared, for everything would be ok." He went on to tell me that he was very excited about seeing his wife again and it would be very soon.

I started talking about the warm weather as we both were rocking in the rocking chairs. Mr. Williams stopped me and asked if I would like to have any of his items, when he leaves.

Mr. Ted Williams 1975

I said to him, "Mr. Williams. You will be here for a little longer, so enjoy your pretty items."

He stopped rocking, looked me right in my eyes and said, "Officer Kittrell. I will not be here tomorrow. My wife has never lied to me. We will be together in the morning.

"Now there was this one time in 1945, my wife and her girlfriends went to a club on U Street to celebrate that the war was over. It was a glorious time; people dancing in the streets, the boys were coming home. My wife had a brother in the army and he had been wounded in Germany, during the battle of the bulge, but he was okay.

"When my wife came home, she smelled like alcohol. She stated that she hadn't been drinking, but I didn't pursue the matter. I was just happy that she was home safely. "

We both started laughing. I told Mr. Williams that I had to go and walk the beat, but I would be back tomorrow and check on him.

He grabs my hand, looks me right in the eyes, as a grandfather to a grandson, and said, "Marco, have a great life. Enjoy your family, for that is what is important in life. After everything is over, that is what you will have at the end. If you are lucky as I was, find that women and love her as nothing else matters."

I just said, "Thanks, Mr. Williams" and walked away. As I walked away I stopped, turned around, and waved at Mr.

Williams. He smiled, waved back, and walked into the house. I said *there goes my friend with the bowtie*. He always wore a bowtie, seven days a week. He always said he would teach me how to tie a bowtie.

The next day I reported to work and learned that Mr. Williams had died in his sleep, quietly, the night before. I was very upset and wanted to go by his house. After roll call, I rushed to his home and saw several people standing on the porch.

As I walked up the stairs, I was greeted by a young man. He immediately grabbed my hand and said, "Good morning, Officer Kittrell. I have been expecting you. My name is John Williams and my grandfather talked about you very much. He always stated that you and he had breakfast once a week. My grandfather really enjoyed that and I want to thank you for being so nice to my grandfather."

I stayed for another hour and spoke with the family. I attended the funeral and during the service I remembered what Mr. Williams told me about his family.

I was very lucky to know Mr. Williams. I missed our talks and times together. He was a good friend and mentor to me. I wish I had more time with him and he had taught me how to tie a bowtie, but I thank God for the time I did have with him. I cried for several days. I miss my friend.

Officer Walter T. Pope
1975
Chapter 6

"A man is only a man but only a man knows a man"
LT Marco F. Kittrell, MPDC, (ret)

I was sitting in roll call working the 7 a.m. to 3: 30 p.m. tour of duty. I was still a rookie and my training officer was off that day. I was wondering whom I would be working with today, in that I wasn't certified to work by myself.

I was fresh out the academy and the older officers were still making fun of me. It wasn't that bad, but just being call kid got to me sometimes. I knew I was only 20, but still, I was a police officer. To these guys it didn't matter if you were 50, once out of the academy you are a rookie and a kid. I just rode that horse.

The roll call sergeants, three of them, enter the room with the lieutenant leading the way. I used to always say, *one day I would be a lieutenant.* My lieutenant was McCoy and he was a big guy with a very big head. He had been on the police force for 25 years and everyone respected the lieutenant. Roll call to me was like a Broadway play. Everything the supervisors did was all planned by them to get a reaction from the troops. But I loved what I saw; professional and proud men.

There was a long table in front of the squad room and only supervisors sat there. The lieutenant always sat in the middle of the table and read the teletype. There was a sergeant at the left and right of the lieutenant and one sergeant sat to the far right. I used to call him the backup man. I don't know why. The sergeant appeared to be canvassing the room for something. I never knew what it was. Even after 40 years, I still don't know what he was looking for. I guess he didn't have anything to do, so he just looked around and acted as if he was looking for something. The strangest thing was that no officer ever looked at him, even the older guys. The sergeant on the right would give the assignments and the sergeant on the left would make all the notifications regarding new information concerning policy changes and other topics of interest.

When the time came to be given your assignment, the sergeant would call your name and the officer would answer, "Yes, Sergeant." When the sergeant got to me, he said, "Kittrell. You are working with Officer Walter T. Pope today."

I said to myself, *God-damn! That sorry mother-fucker!* Officer Pope was a living legion. He had been a police officer for 25 years. Officer Pope knew the streets of Washington, DC, and every criminal in the world. He could tell you by just watching a person if the suspect was wanted for a crime or even carrying a weapon; gun or knife. This used to always amaze me.

The problem with Officer Pope was that he was an alcoholic. He would drink on duty and was always drunk. When he got drunk, he was always out of control. He had been suspended from duty so many times that it was reported that Officer Pope had his own file cabinet at the disciplinary review board; this is where officers' records are stored. But, still, Officer Pope solved criminal cases and always solved the big cases in the police district.

If something happened, the detectives would always call on Pope. Pope knew everyone in the city, especially in the Seventh District where we worked.

Last year a little girl was kidnapped, brutally beaten, and raped. The little girl could describe her attacker. The detectives asked Officer Pope to help and within two hours the attacker was identified, located, and arrested.

The suspect was given a sentence of life, with no parole.

Officer Pope was given a medal by the Mayor.

I was told when Pope arrived for the presentation that he was drunk from the night before so the police department decided to have a private ceremony. Officer Pope was still issued a medal and no pictures were taken. They said that the ceremony was in a hallway.

After roll call, Officer Pope and I entered our police cruiser. As always, I was given a sermon by the veteran police officer.

Officer Pope said, "Rookie sit on the passenger's side. Don't touch the police radio, don't drive, and just be quiet.

As always, I said, "Yes sir."

It was very quiet that morning and Officer Pope started telling me about his life. His wife had left him five years ago and had taken his only child, a little girl named Mary. He admitted that he drank too much and that was the reason for the breakup with his family. The last night they were together, he was drinking and pushed his wife away from him as he was drinking. His wife just wanted him to stop and he wouldn't. He admitted that he loved his wife and didn't mean to push her down to the floor. The worst part was that his little girl observed the whole incident. He really regretted that day and wished he could take it back.

It was a very sad story and I felt bad for Officer Pope. He really needed help with his problem and the department had programs for such issues, but, during that time it wasn't really considered to be a big issue. I didn't know why, but most of the policemen on the job drank too much. It was even considered to be polite when another police officer entered your office and you offered him a drink

We stopped by a church on Morris Road. From this position, you could see most of downtown Washington. It was

Officer Walter Pope 1975

a beautiful sight to see. I said to myself, *Officer Pope must want to have a drink. It is late in the day; 10: 00 a.m. for him that is.*

He surprised me. He started drinking a can of Pepsi soda while looking down on another area. He said that he was attempting to identify the new drug gang members that had taken over the drug area, where they sold heroin in the morning. Heroin dealers normally sell their drugs three times a day for different types of customers. You could learn a lot from Officer Pope, when he was in the mood to teach you how to be a police officer.

Then something happened that only happens once in a million cases. I saw a man pull a woman by her hair into an alley. He had covered her mouth so that she couldn't scream. I immediately attempted to jump out the police cruiser.

Officer Pope grabbed me by my arm and said, "Wait a minute, rookie."

The man then started to beat the women and I again attempted to jump out the car.

Officer Pope said, "I told you, Rookie, wait a minute."

The suspect pulled the woman's pants off and pulled his pants down.

Officer Pope said "Now! Go and lock that mother-fucker up and beat his ass while you are at it. I am right behind you."

I ran down the hill and the suspect never knew what hit him. As he was about to jump on the lady, I jumped on him, and within a few seconds, he was handcuffed. He did put up a fight, but it wasn't much of a fight. He had his pants down. I won.

By this time, Officer Pope got there and said, "Good job, Rookie. I am getting old. I would have just shot the mother-fucker in the head."

The lady lying on the ground said, after I removed the towel from her mouth, "Give me your gun. I will shoot that one-inch mother-fucker in the head. If he hadn't grabbed me from the rear like a little bitch, I would have kicked his ass all over Morris Road; the one-inch mother-fucker."

Once I saw his little dick, I almost started laughing, but didn't want him to get too mad as he was trying to get it up.

Officer Pope grabbed the suspect and said, "Miss. Do you want to hit him, this piece of shit?"

I thought he was kidding. I forgot it was Pope. The lady then hit the suspect in the face.

Officer Pope said, "Okay sir. You are now under arrest."

During the investigation, the lady told us that as she was in the alley getting out of her vehicle, the suspect grabbed hear from the rear and took her to the location where we observed the assault.

Officer Pope later told me that when we first observed the assault, all we had was a simply assault case. The suspect would have walked away from prosecution. But, once he removed the lady's pants and his pants, then we had an attempted rape case which was a better case to prosecute. Pope was right and the suspect was sentenced to 30 years. The suspect was also charged with three other rape cases that had occurred earlier in the year and was found guilty on all three cases. Officer Pope gave me all the credit and I received an award from the police department.

A few years later, I was promoted to sergeant. Officer Pope was sick and in the hospital and I went to visit him. I had this young officer drive me; rank has its privileges. When I walked into Officer Pope's hospital room, I observed this young lady with him.

Officer Pope said, "Hi, Sergeant Rookie, this is my daughter, Mary." I was glad that she had come to see her father. I stayed for about an hour and left.

We gave Mary a ride back to her dorm. She was attending Howard University, Washington, DC, and studying to be a nurse. My driver escorted her to her dorm. When the officer returned to the vehicle, he was smiling. I felt something was up. One year later, Mary graduated from college and married that young police officer.

Officer Pope recovered from his illness, retired from the police department, became a deacon at Mary's church, and he and his wife remarried. Officer Pope stopped drinking. He gave his daughter all the credit for helping him and saving his life. Mary had three children, all boys. The first boy was named Walter Pope after his grandfather.

Mary later told me that her father had paid for her college and established a scholarship for her. All that time, she didn't know where the money was coming from until, when her father first got sick, her mother told her. Officer Pope thought his daughter wouldn't have taken the money because of the hostility that she had against him.

The next few years Officer Pope had a great life and we stayed in touch. I guess time resolves all issues. Officer Pope died in 1998. I think about Officer Pope, even today; a good police officer who had some demons, but they went away at the end. He was a good grandfather; his grandkids loved him very much. They called him Grand Pop, he really like that.

I miss Grand Pop; he wasn't that bad. Smile.

My First Homicide Case
1975
Chapter 7

I had just been certified to patrol by myself and I was assigned to Scout Car 17. It was Monday morning and I felt like a king. I had my police car, everything was going well, and I was full of confidence. It was rush hour and traffic was backed up as usual. But, I didn't care. I was Officer Kittrell. I had just been certified and the world was my kingdom to rule.

I was at the McDonald's on New York Avenue getting my breakfast when the dispatcher directed me to respond to the People's Drug store located on the corner of North Capital and Florida Avenue N.W. It was reported that the manager was lying down on the floor, appearing to be unconscious, and the staff couldn't enter the store. I immediately answered the dispatcher and responded to the location.

On my arrival, I observed four people standing in front of the store saying to me at the same time, "Officer. Mr. Kramer is inside the store and lying down, something is wrong, I believe I see blood." I looked inside the store though the window and confirmed their story. I also observed that a safe was opened. I advised the dispatcher of the situation, kicked the door in, and ran towards the gentleman while telling the employees to stay outside. I immediately observed a bullet hole to Mr. Kramer's head. It was the biggest bullet hole that I have ever observed. I have seen many, but that was the biggest. I couldn't believe my eyes. It appeared that all the blood in his head had drained out and he was looking right at me, with his mouth wide open and his glasses slightly covering his eyes. Mr. Kramer appeared to be over 60 years. I later learned that he was 70 and this was his last year to work. He was training his replacement. He had planned to retire the following month.

By the odor in the store, it appeared that Mr. Kramer had been dead for a while. I kept looking at him. I have never seen such a sight. It was like being in a movie, but this was real and a man had just been murdered.

I removed my weapon and looked around the store for a few seconds, just in case the suspect or suspects were still hiding in the store. It appeared like Mr. Kramer's eyes were following me around the store. It was a very creepy feeling. I went back to my car and gave an update.

I wasn't the politest person on the police radio, in that this was my first murder case and I had just observed a man with a bullet hole in his head. This was the first and last time I acted in this manner.

I could hear the other police units responding and the

ambulance blasting its siren. They sounded good to me. The employees kept asking me if Mr. Kramer was OK. I wanted to say, "Don't you see that big bullet hole to his head and all that blood on the floor. What do you think?" But I didn't.

The other units arrived on scene along with Sergeant Burt Myles, who was a 20-year veteran and a good sergeant. I really liked working with him. He was a hard ass, but a fair hard ass. He told you like it was and you always could tell where he was coming from. He never did act different when he was dealing with you.

The sergeant took me to the side and as I was attempting to tell him what happened, he stopped me. He said, "Officer Kittrell, don't you ever talk the way you did on the radio. Take your time, compose yourself, and then advise the dispatcher of what the hell you got. Not half cocked. Do you understand me, officer?"

I said, "Yes, sir!"

He went on for few more seconds, telling me the correct way to handle the situation. I didn't get too upset, because I always felt that he was a good trainer and he treated everyone fair. He never embarrassed you in front of anyone else. He was a good role model to follow.

Once the homicide detectives arrived, they went right to work. They had me and other officers start canvassing the area for further witnesses. I located a gentleman who was picking up empty cans on the street, walking two blocks from the shooting. I asked if he had seen anything unusual in the area. He never looked at me. He just kept picking up cans. He stated that he just heard that somebody shot and killed Mr. Kramer. Said he was a good man and always helped people in the area when they went into the store. He suddenly stopped and pointed at a house that appeared to be abandoned. Then he ran away, very fast.

I knew this house and no one lived there. I knew junkies used the house to sell and use drugs, but that was always at night, never this early in the day. I called the detectives and informed them what had just happened. I always liked working with the detectives from homicide. They were good and never missed anything. They went over every detail with a fine-tooth comb.

Detective Mark Wilson told me to follow him and we were going to search the house. I asked if we needed a search warrant.

Detective Wilson smiled and said, "If we need one, we will get one. Right now, we don't need one."

As we got closer, two men jumped out the side window and the chase was on. We had several officers in the area and we could catch them quickly, within a block.

As I was about to grab my suspect, he pulled out a Colt 45 and attempted to shoot me. But Detective Wilson struck him to the face, knocking him down to the ground. I didn't know Detective Wilson was so fast.

The detective said, "Kittrell, always remember, the hands are always faster than the eye and always watch those damn hands. It will save your life one day."

I would learn this lesson much later in my career and it did save my life, which is another story. The second suspect was also carrying a firearm and had to be subdued.

Later, the investigation revealed that Mr. Kramer had entered the store at approximately 5 a.m. and the two suspects were hiding in the alley. When Mr. Kramer opened the back door to the store, the two suspects produced hand guns and forced their way in.

Once inside, they forced Mr. Kramer to open the safe. The suspects said they didn't mean to shoot Mr. Kramer but it was an accident. When they pushed Mr. Kramer to the side, after he opened the safe, one of the hand guns they were holding accidently went off and the bullet struck him in the head, killing him instantly. One of the suspects was only 18 years old and the other suspect was 25 years old.

These were two young men who could have selected another life other than selecting a life of crime. Throughout my career this was always something that I could never understand. People can make their own decisions in life. Whenever I saw young people committing such heinous crimes, I was always disturbed by such conduct. We live in such a beautiful world with so many opportunities a person can make. Why chose crime.

I attended Mr. Kramer's funeral. It was very large. I never identified myself as a police officer to the family. It didn't matter who I was. They had lost a father, grandfather, brother, uncle, and husband; someone who kissed his wife that morning and never returned home.

I learned then to love your family, kiss them every day, and appreciate what God Has given you; a family with children.

Ms. Smith

1975

Chapter 8

It was 5:30 p.m. and I had just received an assignment for a burglary and the victim had been assaulted by the suspect. I was the first unit on the scene and when I approached the front door, I was met by an elderly woman who I will call Ms. Smith. She opened the door and I immediately observed that she had been beaten to the face and blood was running down her legs. Ms. Smith then fell in my arms and started crying.

I called for an ambulance and for additional assistance.

Ms. Smith looked at me as if she was looking through me.

She tells me that she entered her kitchen at approximately 9 a.m., after getting out of bed. When she entered the kitchen, she saw a man sitting at her table. This of course stunned her and she couldn't move.

The suspect told her, "Do not scream and you will not be hurt." The suspect then grabbed Ms. Smith, struck her to the face with his fist, threw her down on the floor, and raped her.

After the assault, he stole $200 from Ms. Smith and ran out the back door. Ms. Smith lay on the floor for approximately 10 minutes, crying, before she called the police.

This was the first time that I had seen an elderly person sexually assaulted. It was a very terrifying and disturbing event. I just didn't think a person could commit such a heinous crime against an unprotected woman, especially an elderly woman.

As the ambulance crew was treating Ms. Smith, she started asking for her husband.

I asked, "Ms. Smith. Where can I locate Mr. Smith?"

She replied, "He is at work. He is a fireman."

This sounded very strange to me in that Ms. Smith was 81 years old, and I knew most firemen retired before they reached 61 years or younger.

I called the fire department and after several phone calls I learned her husband died 30 years earlier while combating a house fire. He was on the top floor and the floor caved in, killing him and two other firemen.

Ms. Smith was transported to the hospital where she later died as result of her injuries. Her children and grandsons were Washington, DC, firemen, following in their grandfather's footsteps.

They thanked me for being with their grandmother. They also told me their grandmother was a retired teacher. She was an educator for approximately 50 years and helped many children in the Washington Metropolitan area.

Prior to Ms. Smith's death, she gave a very good description of her attacker. Furthermore, several important pieces of evidence were also recovered, which helped to convict the suspect. Witnesses observed the suspect leaving the home and physical evidence connecting the suspect to the crime scene. The detectives did an outstanding job investigating the crime.

The suspect was later caught and convicted of murder and several other crimes against Ms. Smith. He was sentence to two life terms.

While in jail and a year later, the offender was killed by another inmate who knew Ms. Smith. The inmate was also serving a life sentence for murder. He said Ms. Smith was his school teacher and taught him how to read and write. What was one more killing? He was not getting out of jail. It was also reported that the suspect had been repeatedly sexually assaulted before being stabbed several times.

The Great Dog Chase 1975

Chapter 9

I was walking a foot beat in the 400 block of H Street, Northwest. It was 11: 00 a.m., on a very warm day in July and I was feeling good. Every police officer was on a years' probationary period after graduating from the police academy. If you didn't make the grade, you were fired. I had just passed my probationary year and been certified, which meant I could keep my job and patrol by myself. It made me feel like I was part of the family and everyone had accepted me.

My foot beat consisted of business and residential houses. Every time I walked past a business or someone's home, they would say, "Good Morning, Officer." It made me feel special. My uniform was very neat and all my brass was shining. I was like a king on a horse. I was the man! The young ladies would walk by and smile and I would take off my hat and say, "Good morning ladies" and they would really smile.

I started walking in the 600 block of 4Th Street. It was a residential area with very beautiful homes that were all 60 years old or older. It was at that time when I heard very loud music coming from Mr. Taylor's home.

I knew Mr. Taylor. He was approximately 90 years old. He always nodded his head when I walked past his home, as to acknowledge me, but never spoke. I always wanted to stop and talk with him, but for some reason I never got around to speaking with him, other than saying have a good day. This would be a day that I wouldn't speak of again until writing this book.

Mr. Taylor's music was so loud that people started pointing at his home, as if to say, "Officer. Please tell that man to turn his music down." It was too loud. Every vehicle that drove by the house, the driver would look at Mr. Taylor as to say, "Man is you hard of hearing?"

I approached Mr. Taylor's home and observed him smoking a cigar and stomping his feet to the sounds of BB King. He was also drinking bourbon which was labeled on the bottle, next to his chair. He was having a good time. I was just going to tell Mr. Taylor to turn the music down and advise him that it was against the law to drink alcohol in public. But that wasn't a big issue, in that he was sitting on his front porch. I never suspected what would happen next.

I said, "Good morning Mr. Taylor, could you please turn your music down, the citizens are complaining and they would appreciate if you would comply."

The Great Dog Chase 1975

Mr. Taylor looked at me and said, "I have been living in this house for 60 years, twice as old as you from what I can see. Who in the hell are you to tell me what to do in my own house, you young fucker." Before I could respond, Mr. Taylor said in a very loud voice, "King, come here."

As I looked at the front door, a very large German Shepherd dog appeared and started growling and looking at me.

Mr. Taylor, then said, "Get him."

The dog started running towards me. I started running up the street with the dog right behind me. It was the most humiliating thing I ever experienced. I attempted to stop and shoot the dog, but the animal was right on my heels. I said, "God. Just give me one second and I will shoot this damn dog." But, I didn't have that second. The dog was so close, that if I had stopped the dog would have taken a big bit out of my leg or other part. I wasn't going to let that happen. The chase was only a few seconds, but it appeared to be a lifetime.

The dog chased me for only a half block and then stopped, as I ran across the street, as if to say, "This is my area and you are on my territory. Now get the hell out and don't come back."

I stopped and the dog could have gotten me, but he didn't. The dog just kept looking at me and barking. It was so humiliating. To make things worse, several people who had observed the chase started laughing at me. It was one of the lowest points in my young life.

The dog stopped barking, took its paws and started digging dirt as if to taunt me. It then walked away very slowly. The dog kept looking back at me. It appeared the animal was smiling and laughing at the same time.

I stood there for a few seconds wondering what to do. I wanted revenge on that damn dog and Mr. Taylor. I wasn't going to be run off my foot beat by some old man and his old dog.

After thinking for a few seconds, I said, *I'll call the sergeant.* He was smart and I always looked up to him. He was my supervisor and I felt he would know what to do. The sergeant conducted himself like a real professional and always gave me good advice on the proper way of handling myself as a police officer.

I called the sergeant and shortly thereafter Sergeant John Watkins arrived on the scene. Watkins was a very tall man from the great state of Texas. The sergeant loved being a sergeant and was the ideal Texan. He was my pinup of a Texan.

The sergeant pulled up in his new police cruiser. It was shiny and smelled like a new police car. He exited his vehicle wearing his dark sunglasses. It appeared that it took the sergeant an hour to exit his car, in that he was so tall. He walked towards me, looking like John Wayne as if he had just gotten off a horse. The sergeant also wore black cowboy boots and they were also shining. The most stunning thing about the sergeant, that always amazed me, was that he liked wearing gold and diamond rings with one on each hand. Sometimes the sergeant would have two rings on each hand and the diamonds were big.

The sergeant walked up to me and said, "Kittrell, what do you got?"

I began to tell the sergeant about the incident and I could tell by his face that he was upset.

Before I could finish my story, the sergeant stopped me and said, "Wait one damn minute. You mean to tell me that that old-mother-fucker told a dog to bite you on your ass?"

I said, "Yes sir!"

Sergeant Watkins said, "Don't tell me nothing further. Now, let me tell you something, Kittrell. If you are planning to stay on this police force, you must be your own man, and don't let anybody run you off your beat. Let's go and lock that mother up and if need be, shoot the fucking dog."

Now this made me feel good. I said, "OK sergeant. I'm with you."

I got into the sergeant's cruiser and we drove to Mr. Taylor's home. As we exited the vehicle, Mr. Taylor's cigar fell out of his mouth and he started looking at me right in my eyes. As the sergeant and I reached Mr. Taylor's front gate, Mr. Taylor yelled out, "You son-of a bitch! You went and got the white man on me."

The sergeant immediately said, "Sir, now we don't need comments like that."

Mr. Taylor yelled out, "Butch! King!" Two German Shepherds came running out the house. Mr. Taylor yelled once again, "Get them." Both dogs came running at the sergeant and me. We both started running.

The sergeant was leading the way and that same dog, King, was on my rear end. I couldn't stop running, but the sergeant was in front of me blocking me from going faster.

Sergeant Watkins and I stopped running at the same spot I had originally stopped, when King chased me.

The dogs also stopped at the same spot on the other side of the street where King had stopped when he was chasing me earlier. Both dogs started to bark and began walking away very slowly, as if to say, "Get off our block."

The sergeant said, "Those were some well trained dogs."

I asked the sergeant what we were going to do.

His next statements stunned me, "Kittrell. We will let that old man get his way for now and we will get him later. But whatever you do, don't tell anybody what happened today. That is an order."

This was not what I wanted to hear from my idol.

The sergeant called for another sergeant to pick him up. Before leaving, the sergeant told me to walk another beat and leave Mr. Taylor alone. We will get him later.

Three hours after the sergeant left, he went back and got his vehicle and drove away like a repo man. It was a sad site to see. I didn't hold it against the sergeant. I guess he wanted to handle it in his own way.

We never went back to arrest Mr. Taylor. I guess he was too old to worry about, but my feelings were still hurt.

Two months later, Mr. Taylor died of a heart attack and we had to shoot the dogs to recover Mr. Taylor's body. Even though they had chased me earlier, I felt sorry for the dogs. They were very pretty animals and extremely well trained.

10 years later, Sergeant Watkins retired. At his retirement dinner, I was there.

As they were roasting the sergeant, he looked at me and said," Lt. Kittrell, if you have any pride and respect for my family, please don't tell them about the dogs that chased us that day. I beg you not to; I have nightmares about that day."

I said, OK sergeant. I will take it to the grave." I never told the story again until today.

The sergeant and his wife moved back to Texas and they still live there today. When I retired in 1995, he sent me a post card with him sitting on his front porch with his two dogs named King and Butch, telling me to enjoy my retirement.

He was a great sergeant and later a good friend. He is still livening in the great state of Texas with his wife Betty.

The Great Safe Robbery
1975
Chapter 10

I was patrolling on the Anacostia Freeway at approximately 6 am and driving towards downtown Washington, DC. It was Sunday morning and I had just finished eating breakfast. It was then that I saw the strangest thing, an old blue 1978 Ford with a big black safe tied to the top of the vehicle. Now that will get any policeman's attention!

Furthermore, the safe had been tied down by a rope that was attached to four arms that were extended from a window of the vehicle. Now this looked suspicious, even to Ray Charles. I said to myself, *I know that I am not the first police officer who has seen this unusual sight. It just isn't your normal way to transport a safe.*

I immediately attempted to stop the vehicle, and as soon as I activated my siren and police lights, the vehicle in question started to run. I advised the dispatcher that I had a "fast one" that refused to pull over.

The suspects started to untie themselves from the safe. The driver was first, then the passenger in front, second. The passenger behind the passenger in front was third. The fourth suspect, behind the driver, was slow. As the safe rolled off the vehicle it was the funniest thing I ever seen.

The safe rolled off the vehicle and the fourth suspect, who was slow to release, came out through the window, over the top of the vehicle, still attached to the safe, by-way of the rope.

The safe tumbled over a hill with the suspect closely rolling with the safe. The safe and the suspect both landed in a small body of water. I advised the dispatcher to let the vehicle I was chasing escape. I knew other police vehicles had joined the chase and they would capture the other suspects. I jumped from my vehicle and as I approached the suspect, the safe started to sink.

The suspect began yelling to me, "Save me police officer, please save me."

I knew that the water wasn't that deep and the suspect would not drown. Apparently, the suspect didn't know that. This was now my time to have some fun. I had plenty of time.

I said, "Buddy, it looks like you are not going to make it. Do you have any family you would like for me to contact and tell them what happen?"

The suspect said, "Officer, what kind of man are you? You are the police and you are supposed to protect and serve;

mother-fucker. Save me! You are the damn police! I know that I stole this bitch."

That was enough for me. I didn't want to kill my case by way of his confession. Besides, he might die from shock. I cut the rope, placed handcuffs on the suspect, and walked him up the hill.

As we reached the top of the hill, the safe sunk in the water, just barely. The suspect looked at me and said, "Officer, I almost died in that fucking water and as soon as I get to court I am going to tell the judge every damn thing. I am going to have your job, badge, pension, and every fucking thing."

The suspect fell to the ground, and I realized his arm had been broken or fractured during his ordeal.

I started laughing. All I could see was this professional thief coming out the window and rolling over the car and down that hill with the safe still attached to him. In those days, we didn't have cameras attached to the police vehicles, but it would have made the hall of fame for funny videos.

The other suspects had crashed their vehicle into a pole and rolled over as they attempted to get off the expressway. All three of those suspects were seriously injured, but none of the injuries were fatal. The vehicle had run out of gas as they were making the turn.

Later, the investigation revealed that two days before

payday the suspects had broken into a warehouse in Baltimore, Maryland, which is approximately 50 miles from Washington, DC. The staff of this warehouse was paid on Monday mornings with cash, after the employees received their pay checks. One of the suspects had worked in the warehouse and knew the layout. The security officers guarding the safe were part of the conspiracy.

With the help of a crane, we finally got the safe out the water. The company that owned the safe responded to the scene and opened the safe. During the whole time, the owners were laughing. I assumed they were laughing at the suspect. Once they opened the safe, I started laughing too. The safe was empty.

The company had changed their payday and the employees were paid the previous Friday.

The trial is another story. The jury laughed so hard, they couldn't get though the proceeding. Even the judge had a good laugh and he never laughed at anything. Even you must laugh at the Great Safe Robbers.

Smile.

The Jungle
1975
Chapter 11

It was approximately 7:30 p.m. and my partner Michael Gray and I were patrolling in the 3300 block of South Capitol Street, Southeast. It was at that time two females ran to our vehicle while we were stopped at a traffic light. Both ladies were later identified as Ms. Robin Williams and Ms. Cathy Scott. They were both bleeding profusely in the face and head area.

They were both hysterically talking at the same time. They said that they had just been robbed and beaten by two suspects while standing at the bus stop. The suspects were both armed with sawed-off shot guns.

Michael told the ladies to get in the vehicle and we started searching for the suspects. I was in the process of informing the dispatcher when, Ms. Scott stated, "There are the motherfuckers that robbed and beat us."

They were walking very slowly. When the suspects saw us, they immediately bolted and ran into a wooded area. Mike and I exited our vehicle and gave chase. Once we reached the wooded area, I gave chased after one suspect and Michael chase the other suspect. In other words, we separated which was not a smart move on our parts. We were both young and had only one year on the job.

By this time, it was very dark and my heart was beating a hundred miles a minute. I could still see the suspect as he was running in the woods. He was carrying what appeared to be a sawed-off shotgun. The whole time I am thinking, *I am going to get my man and he wasn't going to get away from me!* Especially after seeing those two ladies beaten in the manner they were. It was then when I slipped over a rock and fell to the ground.

I immediately jumped up and pulled my weapon, thinking that the suspect might attempt to shoot me. I started looking around very slowly, realizing that I had lost sight of the suspect. I didn't want to get shot or killed while in the woods. It suddenly got darker and I realized that I was by myself and couldn't see my hands. I got very concern, because I was in the woods with two suspects armed with shotguns. My partner probably, with his weapon out, was in the same predicament. It was the place the senior officers always told me not to ever be. My training just went out the window. I was in a jam.

I could hear the sirens of other police units responding to the scene. But, at that time, it sounded as if they were a thousand miles away.

I knew of several police officers being shot or killed by

suspects or, even worse, their own partners by not knowing the position of each other and the suspects; especially in the dark. *Damn fool!*

I saw a glimpse of light. I started walking towards it believing it would lead me out of what looked like a jungle at the time. I then heard a cracking sound. I stopped and fell to the ground. It was a damn cat. It scared the crap out of me. The cat stopped, looked at me as if to say, "You are stupid to be chasing two men, armed with shotguns, into a wooded area in the dark." The cat walked away very slowly, looking back at me, as to say, "Good luck, Stupid. I can see in the dark, can you?" I should have followed the cat out.

I then heard a police helicopter and they started to light up the area with their lights. It made me feel better, but I knew it would probably make the suspects nervous and might force their hand. I wasn't in a position to get in a gun battle. By me not thinking, I had left my police radio in the police cruiser so I couldn't communicate with anyone. As I got closer to the light I glimpsed earlier, I saw it was coming from a street light, but the area was fenced in and I couldn't get out. I did see that damn cat walking down the street and it stopped and looked back at me. The cat probably said *that is one stupid police officer, looking like he needs help.* The cat then ran away. Like I said, I should have followed the damn cat.

I retraced my footprints, walking very slowly. I then heard a voice from the perimeter of the woods telling me to come out the woods. I said to myself, *what the hell you think I am trying to do? If I knew the way-out, I would have been out the damn woods.*

I heard the voice again and I recognized the voice as Lieutenant John McCoy. The lieutenant kept saying, "Kittrell, walk towards my voice." This saved me.

Within a few seconds I found my way out of what I have forever called, "The Jungle." When I reached the perimeter, all I could see was police officers and police dogs. It looked like the entire police department was there and everyone was looking at me, as to say, "What the hell where you are thinking about, Rookie?"

I walked towards Lieutenant McCoy. Officer Gray who was standing next to him and the lieutenant said, "Kittrell, Stand next to Mike."

The lieutenant asked the sergeant if his men were in place. The sergeant had positioned officers completely around the wooded area.

The sergeant said, "Yes, Sir."

During those times, the Metropolitan Police Department didn't have many black lieutenants, but the ones they did have, were damn good. Lieutenant McCoy was an experienced lieutenant and he knew his stuff. He's from the old school of policing and went by the book. He was respected by everyone. I wanted to be like Lieutenant McCoy.

He ran this operation like his army was about to invade an island. The lieutenant told the helicopter to light the woods completely up. The lieutenant then used the blow horn and told the suspects that, if they didn't come out of the woods, he was going to send the police dogs in and he had "plenty of them."

The whole time he is smoking one of those stinking cigars that he smoked.

Approximately one minute later, the two suspects yelled out, "Hold up police we are coming out. Don't send in the dogs."

The lieutenant replied, "Come out walking, very slowly, with your hands up. Leave your weapons on the ground. The dogs will find them."

Seconds later, the suspects walked out as instructed. They looked like crap and were shaking, as if they were freezing. It was 90 degrees that night.

The lieutenant told the sergeant to arrest those two gentlemen and send in the dogs and locate the weapons. He then told Mike and me to get in his police cruiser. I knew what was coming, a royal chewing out.

Once in the vehicle the lieutenant told us exactly what we did wrong and what we should have done. "Advise the dispatcher before pursuit. Take your damn radio. Never split up; especially at night. Police have died by making those mistakes." He was right and I always learned from the lieutenant. I only hated those stinking cigars he smoked. The windows were rolled up, air condition was blasting, and he must have smoked two of those damn things.

But everyone respected the lieutenant because he was good at his job. He came up the hard way on the job, and he always told the young guys the way things should be done when doing police work. After the chewing out, the lieutenant said. "Now you fine police officers can get the hell out my police cruiser and process your arrest. Can you handle that little detail?"

We said, "Yes sir."

As we exited the vehicle, he said he was glad we weren't hurt or killed. He said he was planning on taking Ms. McCoy on a cruise next week for her birthday and if we had been killed, he would have felt bad while he was on his cruise. But, he was still going since it was paid for in full.

"We said yes sir" and walked away.

While processing the suspects, one of them told me he had seen me several times walking through the woods and could have shoot me at anytime, but he wasn't going to shot a police officer. That wasn't in the cards. He was just as scared as I was. I thanked him for not shooting me. Both suspects pled guilty and were sentenced to five years for armed robbery and assault with a deadly weapon.

When I was promoted to lieutenant years later,

Lieutenant McCoy came to my promotion ceremony. I was very proud and honored that he attended. I had no idea that he was aware that I had gotten promoted. The lieutenant and his wife had relocated to North Carolina. He was still smoking those damn stinky cigars.

I learn a great lesson that day from the lieutenant and he was always there years later to advise me.

Thanks Lieutenant McCoy.

He is still in North Carolina smoking those damn stinky cigars.

Cadillac Jim
1975
Chapter 12

I had been a police officer for approximately 15 months and I felt good about myself. I was certified to patrol by myself and I felt I could handle most assignments. It was Monday and like most Mondays the department was short staffed; days off, officers on leave, and officers attending court. On those days, I knew I would be patrolling by myself, which the police department classified as a 10-99 unit.

It was at approximately 9:30 a.m. and Sergeant Jim Allen called for me and several other units to meet him at South Capitol Street and Atlantic Avenue S.E. When I arrived, Sergeant Allen informed me that he was establishing an entry team to arrest a dangerous suspect whose street name was Cadillac Jim.

I knew of Cadillac. He was a serious gangster who robbed the Washington, DC drug gangs of money, guns, and illegal drugs, especially heroin. It was believed that he had shot and killed nine people, during robberies, in five years. He was a one-man crime wave and his only victims were criminals themselves. It was later learned that he robbed banks. He robbed banks in other jurisdictions when money was tight. That way, local authorities wouldn't connect him to any of the shootings in Washington, DC. But, that is another story.

The drug gangs had hired two hit men from New York City to kill Cadillac, but Cadillac ended up killing the two hit me. This was one of the few men I encountered during my police career of whom I was really concerned, if I had to confront him. When the detectives talked about Cadillac, I understood them. It was with much concern that we executed our orders to the letter. In that way, no one would get hurt. Cadillac was a man who you didn't take lightly. It even sounded like they respected him as a professional criminal. Cadillac never took any unnecessary chances.

Sergeant Allen informed the officers on the scene that a witness was going to give a signal that Cadillac was inside. The entry team would enter the apartment and, once the witness was safe, would attempt to take Cadillac, alive, if possible. I later learned that the witness was Cadillac's girlfriend, Susan, and she was turning him in for the reward money.

Cadillac was taking care of Susan. He was paying her rent and car note. Susan asked Cadillac to pay her rent and car note for a year in advance instead of month to month. Susan also wanted $10,000 in cash, just in case Cadillac went to jail. To that, Cadillac said, "No!"

Sergeant Allen told me that my assignment was to guard

the rear door to the apartment in which Cadillac was hiding. As the entry team was being established, I felt proud that Sergeant Allen had enough faith in me to assume such an important assignment. Officer Wayne Jenkins was at the other end of the hallway guarding that exit.

Sergeant Allen further told me that I would be there for approximately 15 minutes, before the entry team would be in place to execute the search and arrest warrants. This made me feel better about my assignment. I had never seen the detectives so nervous about a person before, which made me very uneasy about Cadillac.

That day taught me a lot about police work. While stationed on my post at the exit of the building, I looked down the hallway every few seconds to make sure Cadillac wasn't walking down the hallway towards me.

I will admit I was border-line scared. In my mind I said, *if the hit men from New York City and the drug gangs are afraid of this man, how am I supposed to feel? Very concerned.*

I didn't know it then, but I learned later that professional criminals are good at what they do and they can smell when something is wrong or out of place.

Maybe it was the way that Susan left the house or maybe it was too quiet. The police had started moving people out of the area. I must say, in that neighborhood and that time of day, there is normally a lot of noise and people moving around.

It was like Death Valley, completely dead. This stillness made Cadillac very nervous, he told me later.

By me being so inexperienced and nervous, I made a big mistake that could have cost me my life. I entered the hallway. I wanted to see if I could hear any movement in the apartment. That wasn't my job.

It was at that time Cadillac exited the apartment and looked right into my eyes. He was wearing silk black pin-striped pajamas. I couldn't believe that I had made such a stupid mistake. Cadillac looked 10 feet tall. When he looked at me, it was as if he looked right through me. I froze. He was there for only three seconds. I don't know why I didn't hear him at the door. Cadillac walked back into his apartment, very slowly, and closed the door, very slowly. This was a mistake I would never make again, if God allowed me to live through this day.

I tried to radio Sergeant Allen to let him know what just happened, but my radio battery must have died. That was another mistake that I wouldn't make again. I didn't check the battery before taking the assignment. The good Sergeant Allen told us to check our radios and I failed to properly check mine.

I started walking backwards to take cover behind the doors between Cadillac's apartment and the stairwell. My gun was still in my holster. I didn't make it.

Cadillac walked back into the hallway, very slowly, but this time he had a 45 Colt in his waist band. He looked at me and said, "Draw."

This scared the living shit out of me. I just knew I was going to die that day. I couldn't move. The police department had trained me very well, but not for this. I was 20 years old and I felt my life was about to end. Cadillac was looking right into my eyes. If I had made any sudden movement, I knew he was going to fire his weapon. I was trying to recover and deal with the threat. My feeling was, *if Cadillac wanted to shoot me; he would have discharged his weapon by now.*

Seconds went by and I had decided to draw, but my weapon was holstered and attached to my holster. *Can I unbutton the holster fast enough to shoot Cadillac? I wasn't going to die without a fight.* I guess God said. "It wasn't my time" and I had a long life to live.

That was when God and I started our long history of having conversations during times of crisis.

Seconds later, four police officers burst into the hallway armed with shot guns pointing them down range in my direction, shouting, "Down to the floor Cadillac!"

I knew they were going to say it only one time and then they would fire those damn shotguns. I also knew that they had loaded the shotguns with rounds and those rounds would go right through anything. They wanted to put Cadillac down and fast, no second chances. Cadillac was like a cool poker player. He looked at the police officers for about two seconds and slowly dropped to the floor, buckling his knees, with his hands pointing in the air. Cadillac then looked at me, for some reason, as he was lying on the floor in the hallway, as if to say, "Kid, you are damn lucky, so damn lucky. Your number was almost called and I was the one calling.

I have never been so damn scared in my life! God gave me a second chance. The police officers, after securing, handcuffing and removing Cadillac from the hallway, asked if I was okay. One thing about being a Metropolitan Police Officer was that when things happened everybody cared about you.

Once I got to the police district, I was really shaken up. But the older officers always told me; when you arrest people, talk to them. Criminals love to talk to police officers after they have been arrested. They are always thinking about their future and maybe they can establish a relationship with the officer. Some criminals considered themselves as professionals and want to be treated as such, especially Cadillac.

I walked into the detective office. Cadillac was sitting in a chair and the detectives were treating him like a king, asking Cadillac, "Do you want some smokes? Coffee?" They even let him order a steak and cheese from Cadillac's favorite carry-out, Miles Long Restaurant, on Martin Luther King Avenue, S.E. Cadillac sat in the chair as if it was a throne and the detectives were his subjects. But, I knew it was a game. If the detectives treated Cadillac in that manner, he would talk to them. They knew Cadillac had nothing to lose. It was all about information into the world that only Cadillac knew.

The senior officers always told the young officers, when given the opportunity, talk to the people you arrest. Criminals might do dumb things, but most of them aren't stupid and policemen can learn from them. Criminals just want the police to respect them as what they are.

This fact might be hard for some people to understand, but police officers and criminals knew well how the game is played when dealing with each other. There is a code of understanding and if police officers want to be successful in their field, they must learn that code of respect.

I am not saying that police officers admire the criminal world. They are just trying to understand their enemy better, because the more you know about them, the more successful you will be when again confronted with your adversary.

From 1950 through 1990, criminals trained each other in the art of committing crime, especially bank robbery. This was a fine art. Cadillac came from this period. This I knew and I also knew that I could learn from Cadillac concerning hard core criminals.

I wanted to talk to Cadillac, but I was hesitant. I didn't want to make a fool of myself when talking with him. Cadillac came from an era where criminals are trained to read people. I wanted him to see me as a police officer and not a rookie. I also wanted to find out why he approached me in the hallway in the manner he did.

I walked over to Cadillac, identified myself as Officer Marco Kittrell, and asked if I could talk with him. Even with that approach, I felt somewhat uncomfortable. I was the police and I am asking him if he would talk to me. I later learned that this was the right approach.

If you get in the habit of going hard, you will be treated likewise. People like Cadillac don't respect officers who go hard, especially a young police officer. When an officer goes hard he learns nothing and therefore is unsuccessful in his pursuits.

Cadillac looked at me as he was smoking a Kool Cigarette, as to indicate that he was in complete charge of the situation. I was attempting to act as if I was a veteran police office. That was a mistake.

If you want information, you must give some information. Cadillac asked if I was a rookie. I said, "No," which was another mistake. By lying, I established that I was dishonest and not being truthful with him. These things I learned later in my career through dealing with people like Cadillac. I am not saying police officers shouldn't lie when interviewing suspects or witnesses, but this wasn't the time.

Cadillac would see through that and this was about respecting one another and establishing ground rules. I just broke one.

Cadillac said, "Okay," while smoking his cigarette.

I said, "Cadillac, Why did you do what you did in the hallway when you saw me? Most wanted people just want to get away." I wanted to hear from Cadillac in his own words the reason for his actions, I wanted to learn.

Cadillac looked at me again, right in my eyes. His words are with me today and established the way I conducted myself as a police officer for the next 45 years.

"Officer Kittrell, I am 40 years old and I have been in these streets for 30 plus years. I know the streets and they aren't pretty. I have been in and out of jail in the last 20 years. I know the system, and the system is always guaranteed to do the same thing when confronted with the same circumstance. When dealing with people like me, it treats me like shit.

"I have maybe 13 bodies, homicide cases, to my name that the police are going to try and pin me with."

(Note: We had possibly nine cases that we were looking at. He just added 4 more). It wasn't a confession. He was fishing. I knew that from listing to the conversation between Cadillac and the detectives. The five detectives had moved to the other side of the office and acted like they weren't listening, but they were to every word.

Cadillac further stated, "When I came out the apartment and saw you, after looking at your face, I knew that I had you. You were scared and I was going to go through you.

"People like me read people very well. It is our trade and we are good at. If I would have been on my game, I would have been long gone before you entered the hallway.

"I knew something was wrong as soon as that bitch left the apartment. I know women and they are some selfish mother-fuckers. You hear me officer? I go by her crib three times a week; eat, shower, and get laid. That is all I need. I only have one woman; anymore and you got problems. That bitch always does the same thing when I get there; like clockwork, shower, eat, get laid, and give her money.

"When I get out the shower, that bitch said, 'Baby I am going to the store to get some soda and beer.' Right then I should have moved my ass faster. It was out of place, totally. I started putting my clothes on. That bitch is about time and she doesn't have that much with me. Therefore, when I am there, all that bitch talks about is money, money, and more money. I should have given that money to her that she wanted. I don't blame her. Business is business and a women's time is limited. I played that number wrong. It will not happen again.

"As I was putting my clothes on, it just goes got-damn quite. That is a very loud neighborhood, especially at that time of the day. Also, the children were not in front of the window playing. That is why I got that apartment. I can see everything and I can get out fast through the door that you were supposed to be watching."

We both started laughing, I don't know why. Cadillac made me feel relax by explaining his actions and I was learning.

"When it got too quiet, I knew the police were about to make their move on me. I heard you walking in the hallway. Police shoes are very loud especially when you are trying to be quiet in an old hallway. I don't know if you know that. Again, that's one of the reasons why I lived there. The hallway is never that quiet. It was early in the morning. Children are always running in and out. Again, that is why I selected that apartment building and children were my alarm clock. The police had only one way in and that was the front door. The back door was too small and police like plenty room. I had a plan to get out.

"There was also a window in the basement that you must know about. That window leads to another apartment and to another and to another. Did you know that, Officer Kittrell?"

"No, I didn't."

"Also, I could get into other apartments. It's like a maze down there, just like you are in a bunker." Cadillac started smiling to himself.

"In addition, it was Monday and the police department is short of people on Monday, Friday, Saturday, and Sunday. I know this. I was surprised that your people could move so quickly. You must have quite a few older and experience policemen working. That is unusual for a Monday. I thought I would have enough time. That was another mistake on my part.

"Like I said, when I saw you, I knew you were scared. I don't want to shoot a police officer. There is no game in that, nothing but hard time. Police don't like it when you shoot their own; it's a police thing. But, when it comes down to it, if it is me or you, I will select me. Police are not trained to draw, you know that, and I was dealing with a young police officer. No disrespect is intended, Officer Kittrell.

"But, when those four white police officers came in that hallway and pointed those damn shotguns at me, they were going to kill me and you too." He pointed his cigarette at me and again started smiling. You were in the line of fire, you know that? Right, Officer Kittrell?"

"Yes, I do."

"I figured I could get by you, but with those four white officers with shotguns I was a dead man. In those few seconds I said to myself, *I was going to lose that battle but hell, I may beat the case.*

"Officers misplace evidence, make mistakes during the trial, or maybe the attorney might offer me a deal and I do about 15 years, but I get out. Hell, make a deal and give up a few of those drug boys that I know is dealing in heroin. Attorneys love deals. But you, Officer Kittrell, was about to meet your maker. I would have tried to wound you if I could, but I didn't have time to mess with you all damn day. I was on the move. You know what I mean, officer? It was only business, nothing personal, just had to get the hell out of there.

"Officer Kittrell, if you are planning to stay on this job, don't ever show fear again. People like me can smell it like garbage, it stinks and smells bad.

"Like I said, I didn't want to shoot you, but I had nothing to gain but hard time and grief, if it means anything to you.

"I never hurt a police officer in my life. You all have always treated me OK, even when you all beat my ass when I was a young puppy in those streets. I was wrong. I grew up fast. Why make trouble for yourself? The police aren't the enemy. It is people like me and we eat each other, always have and always will.

"Officer Kittrell, is there anything else that you would like to ask me? It is getting late. By the time I get to the jail house, it will be dinner time. Today is Monday and they are serving chicken, fried, my second favorite food.

"Also, tell Susan don't worry. It was just business and she made her play. I should have paid my baby. The pussy was very good. You should try it! No, you don't look like the type. Were you a boy scout, Officer Kittrell?"

I said, "Yes."

"I figured. So, we are ok?"

I said, "Yes'" again and walked away.

Before I left the office, I heard the detective say, that if Cadillac would have shot Officer Kittrell, the police would have shot his ass with every shot they had.

Cadillac said, "I know, but after the first shot, it doesn't matter, you are fucking dead. What the hell."

Cadillac was right. The prosecuting attorney offered him a deal and he was sentence to 30 years without the possibility of parole. Cadillac served 5 years and the drug boys finally got him after all the shit that he had put them through for the last 6 years in Washington, DC. Cadillac was serving time in Montana and it was rumored that the drug gangs in Washington, DC, hired some people in prison to kill him. They stabbed Cadillac fifty times. Before then, he was in protective custody. I never learned what happen to take him out of protective custody.

Cadillac taught me a lot in that thirty-minute conversation we had back in 1976. I have been scared many times in the last 40 years, but I have only shown being scared once and that was with Cadillac in that hallway. It seems like it was yesterday, but that conversation saved my life on many occasions. I know it has.

I am so glad that I met the people that had the fortune of meeting during my police career. I took pieces from everyone and put it together. I really appreciated Cadillac talking to me and "schooling me on the streets," as we say, even though he was about to shoot my ass. As he said, "It was only business" if you look at it from his point of view.

That is why whenever I meet another police officer and they tell me that they have never been scare before during their career, I just look at them and say OK. I tell them all I have been scared many times during my career, but only showed it once.

Cadillac had a son and his son joined the Metropolitan Police Department in Washington, DC. I met him years later. I never told him this story about his father. He said that he never knew his father. Susan was his mother. Maybe I should have, I don't know. His son was very happy being a police officer and doing very well. I kept tabs on him during his career. He made it. He was promoted to sergeant in 1995, got married to another police officer, and had two kids.

I know Cadillac is smiling and possibly said, "How did that happen?"

The Parking Lot
1976
Chapter 13

Officer Wayne Scott was a young officer that had many demons. He and I had graduated from the police academy together, only a year earlier. He was a good officer, but had many problems.

While in the police academy, he was going through a divorce and always complained about money. He hated his wife and accused her of adultery. They had been married for 2 years and had gotten married when they were only 18 years old. I couldn't say anything. I got married when I was only 17 years old.

Wayne and I became good friends while in the police academy and even studied together. I always invited him to my house. I never like going to his home. Janice, his estranged wife would stop by the apartment, unannounced, and start arguments. My goal was to become a police officer, not lose my job because of something stupid someone else might do.

Wayne, to me, wasn't the strongest man when dealing with his wife. He still loved her and wanted her to return home. Therefore, whatever she did, he accepted it. It wasn't my marriage or problem. I just wanted to go on and not be associated with the trouble.

They did get back together once he graduated from the academy. They attempted to make it, but his wife started dating other men again. Wayne just couldn't take anymore and asked her to leave their home. But, Wayne was still in love and while working together, I really worried about him.

One day, I could tell that Wayne was very worried. He didn't talk very much. I attempted to start a conversation, but Wayne never responded. After a few hours, I just gave up and gave him his space.

At the end of the day, as Wayne and I were about to get off duty, I invited Wayne to my house for dinner. Wayne said he was fine and he just wanted to go home and rest. We talk a little longer and agreed to meet for lunch tomorrow.

That night, another police officer called me at home. He informed me that Wayne had committed suicide while sitting in his vehicle in the police parking lot, as we called it. This lot was where all the police officers parked their personal vehicles. It was located at 13Th & Mississippi Avenue, Southeast. Apparently, after speaking with me, Wayne went to his vehicle, inserted an eight-track, the Dells, and started drinking some beer.

Several police officers observed Wayne, as they walked by, in the vehicle, but didn't think that anything was wrong. Wayne waved as the officers went by and everything appeared to be OK. As Officer Price was about to enter his vehicle he observed Wayne placing his service revolver in his mouth. Before Officer Price could say anything, Officer Wayne pulled the trigger, killing himself instantly. The bullet went through his head and out the back window of the vehicle, lodging in a tree.

Learning of Wayne's death really disturbed me. That was the last time that I walked away from a friend who I felt was under some type of pressure.

It was Wayne's decision to committee suicide, but I learned later in my police career that sometimes people reach out to you before they commit suicide.

I remember when the technicians removed the bullet from the tree the next day. The technician was laughing as he removed the bullet. That really hurt me to see another police officer acting in the manner that he was. Most police officers didn't respect another officer when they committed suicide. It was just how police officers acted at the time, not all, just the stupid ones.

Once the officer removed the bullet, he said, "Add this to the file with the other losers," and threw the bullet to his partner who in turn placed the bullet in his pocket. They both got in their car, started talking about where they wanted to eat, and drove off.

Wayne's car was still on the scene. No one even cleaned the vehicle or removed the glass that had been shattered when the bullet exited the vehicle. The crime scene was eventually attended too, but they didn't rush. It was like the department was ashamed.

Over the years, the police department did change its attitude concerning officers when they committed suicide. The department accepted its role and began addressing problems that police officers are confronted with that could lead an officer to suicide. That was a good thing and I respected the department for their courage or common sense.

Wayne had a very big funeral, but his estranged wife didn't attend. The bullet hole is still in the tree after all these years. I have visited the tree on several occasions.

The technician that removed the bullet from the tree and laughed as he was performing his job, committed suicide five years later after his wife left him for another police officer.

My mother called me several days later after the funeral. She knew that Wayne and I were friends. She made small talk. It made me feel better. A mother's love is always there, even as a police officer. I miss those talks with my mother. She was such a comfort to me while on the force. I have no problems admitting that.

The Man that changed my Life
1976
Chapter 14

"I am a man and no man can make me lesser than a man"
LT Marco F. Kittrell, MPDC, (ret)

I was 21 years old and ready to conquer the world. I loved being a police officer and wanted to be a good police officer, if not the best that I could be. I had just graduated from the police academy 6 months prior and recently certified to patrol alone as an officer, I was so excited.

It was Saturday night and we were very busy. I started my shift at 3p.m. and worked until my shift was over. I must have handled 40 radio assignments, if not more. My section had only 1 sergeant working in my sector, there were three sectors in the police district. The sergeant's name was Randy Johnson. He was a dreadful sergeant and he was always drunk, sloppy drunk. All the lieutenants and captains knew it, but they were all friends and drank together. What could you do?

On this night, Sergeant Johnson was not only intoxicated but wanted to supervise everyone. He only picked on the young officers. The older officers knew the sergeant and he knew them. It was like an understanding, you may be a sergeant, but don't forget where you came from, we know you, that is another story.

Normally I would see the sergeant on a Saturday night approximate 3 or 4 times during the shift and that was a lot. This shift, I must have seen the sergeant almost every hour. That was because of the work load. We kept running into each other going to and from radio assignments. I said to myself, *the sergeant was tasting again.* But, he could function. I think the action kept him going and prevented him from falling out. I didn't like or respect the sergeant, but he could handle emergencies when they occurred. I will give him that.

At one point during the shift, the sergeant was driving his vehicle and entering a parking lot to back up another police officer on a radio assignment. I don't know what happen, but his vehicle went into a ditch as he was attempting to maneuver the turn. Luckily there weren't any citizens in the area, other than the person that was arrested for driving while intoxicated.

When the sergeant exited his vehicle, the suspect said, "That is the man you should be arresting. Shit, he drinks more than me." The other officer on the scene and I said nothing. We just felt embarrassed.

The Man That Change My Life 1976

At the end of each shift, police officers check in with their supervisor and they approve your police reports and the tickets that you had written during the shift. We call this check off. Tonight's check off would change my life as a police officer.

Sergeant Johnson looked at me as I walked into the room. He told me to wait and see him last. He wanted to talk with me. I waited approximately 15 minutes. The room smelled like a bar because the sergeant had been drinking all night.

After the last officer had been approved to leave for the day, the sergeant told me to close the door, which I did. It was at that time that the sergeant cut into me like a knife through butter.

The sergeant started by saying that I was a "lousy police officer" and I "wasn't doing my job." I should, "consider taking another job, maybe driving a bus or delivering mail." If it was up to him he would have "fired me last year."

Now my first thoughts were that he was just drunk, but still a sergeant and could hurt my career. It would be my word against his and he was in the clique and all the top brass liked him. Why? I didn't know. I just stood my ground and didn't lose my cool. I figure the sergeant wanted me to lose my temper and he would have some reason to suspend me. I wasn't going to play that game. I was young, but not stupid.

The sergeant continued to belittle me and tell me how stupid I was. The words hurt. They hurt very badly. I was young and easy to bruise, but God was with me and he helped me maintain my composure. This went on for approximately 15 minutes. The sergeant found every word to degrade me, but I didn't budge. He wasn't getting my job. I worked too hard to get it and I wasn't going let this drunk take it away from me.

After the sergeant finished - I guess he got tired or that he exhausted his entire vocabulary and couldn't think of any other worlds to speak that would degrade me - he told me that I was free to go and after I get home I should think about what he had said.

When I walked out into the hallway, I saw four other police officers standing next to the door. I knew they heard every world that the sergeant had spoken. They looked at me if to say, "That guy will not be here very long."

I walked to my locker, changed my clothes and left for the day. The words that the sergeant had used really hurt. It was a long drive home and all I could see was that drunken sergeant talking down to me and those other police officers laughing.

I got home, took a long shower, and started to drink some rum. After the second glass, I stopped. I started thinking about my mother and what she had told me when I was young. "Don't you ever let a person dictate to you what to do."

I lay on the sofa and started thinking again about what happened today. After two hours, I concluded that I was a better man than that drunken sergeant. He wasn't going to achieve his goal of making me feel sorry for myself or stop me from becoming a better man than he said I was.

I went to work the next day and Sergeant Johnson said, "Good afternoon, Kittrell. I hope you learned something from what I said last night."

I looked at the sergeant and said, "I did!" and walked away.

For the next twelve months, I studied to get promoted to sergeant. I studies every day and night, when I was in court, weekends, and every other possible minute. Sergeant Johnson started a fire in me and it would not go out.

The sergeant stopped harassing me for a while, but every now and then he would say some smart remark to keep the screws in me. It only made me stronger and smarter.

The following year the sergeant examination was given and I took the test. Not many people encouraged me to take the test, but those that did were the encouragement I needed to get what I wanted. When I took the sergeant's examination, I was answering the questions before I finished reading them. I learned that day that if you wanted it bad enough, you can get it. I did very well on the test.

The second part of the examination was the assessment board. I also did very well and was promoted five months later. Sergeant Johnson never said congratulation. I never expected the same. He did look at me as to say, "I can't believe it" and "I knew he could do it. I couldn't keep him down."

Two years later, I was promoted to lieutenant and reassigned to the Seventh District. Guess who was assigned as one of my Sergeants? Randy Johnson! When I arrived at the district, my captain gave me my section of 28 officers and four sergeants. The sergeant retired that day even before we could have our meeting to discuss the section.

I detested Sergeant Johnson, but I didn't have a mean streak in me for revenge. I wasn't raised that way. I would have treated him the way I wanted to be treated. The sergeant wouldn't have received any favors from me, but I would have been fair.

Three years later, I was the commander of the vice unit handling drug, gambling, and prostitution enforcement at the Seventh District. I really enjoyed the job. You had to be good to arrest people who made a career out of committing vice crimes.

We were working one Friday evening on a sunny day that was also pay day. I told the troops, "Give me several arrests for prostitution and solicitation for prostitution and we will call it a day and go home early." Normally a sergeant will take the troops out and run the operation. On this day I gave all the sergeants the day off and I took the troops out. I said, "Ok, We will arrest some Johns - men who solicit prostitutes for sex - today."

So, I went to the patrol section and got the youngest and prettiest police women. I told them to wear the shortest pants - hot pants - they had because they were going to work on the block.

After they were trained and instructed in how the operation was going to work, we started the maneuver. Within a short time we had several arrests and cars were lined up. During this type of procedure, police officers are instructed to give signals when they arrest certain people like politicians, clergymen, and others with similar back grounds. They still go to jail, but we just like to know who we are dealing with.

I was about to close the operation down, when one of the officers gave me the signal. I said *it had to be the day that I was out here working*. I walked over to the car. The officers said they had arrested a retired MPDC police officer and he was sitting in the back seat of the police cruiser, handcuffed.

I said, "Well, this retired officer is going to jail." I looked in the car and it was Sergeant Randy Johnson. He looked like horse crap. He smelled like a gallon of scotch, not shaven, and wearing clothes like he just got out of the bed. He really looked bad.

He looked right in my eyes and I look back at him and all the hate came back as if it was yesterday. I guess God was testing me again. I had this son of a bitch by the balls. He wouldn't go to jail or lose his retirement, but the embarrassment would kill him.

The arresting officer looked at me and said, "Lieutenant, I think I made a mistake, I don't believe I have sufficient probable cause to arrest him." All the other officers agreed.

I look back at the sergeant and said, "Ok, let him go." Sergeant Johnson exited the police cruiser and the handcuffs were removed. He rubbed his arm as if the handcuffs were too tight and caused some discomfort.

He walked away with his head hanging down and never said a word to me or the other police officers. All the officers that were working were young. They didn't recognize the sergeant as he had retired before they arrived at the police district.

As the sergeant walked away, all the hate I had for that man walked away with him. I asked God then to give me the strength to never hate a man the way that I hated the sergeant. Hatred takes away from you, shortens your life, and makes you a weaker person.

Sergeant Johnson attempted to break a young man, myself, several years earlier and it was the best thing that ever happened to me. He gave me the motivation and reason for being the best police officer that I could be.

Sergeant Johnson was killed several years later in Baltimore by a prostitute with a knife. She slashed his throat and he bled to death before the police arrived.

It was reported by the police that the sergeant had been in the alley for approximately 5 hours before someone found him. I went to his funeral and said a prayer for him. There weren't many people at the funeral, not even his drinking friends.

My Best Friend
1976
Chapter 15

"You are my friend until the end and may that end never come again."
LT Marco F. Kittrell, MPDC, (ret)

Officer Clarence Jacobs and I were the best of friends. We were police cadets together. We entered the police academy on the same day and graduated on the same day. At the time, we were very close and I felt he was my dearest friend.

One fine day in June, we left work early, at approximately 11:00 a.m. Clarence wanted me to help him move some furniture from his apartment into storage. He and his girlfriend had decided to live together and get married the following year.

Clarence was very happy and much in love with his girlfriend, Mary. They had been dating for two years. Clarence wanted to get married and have children while he was young. I have never seen him so happy. I was glad for my friend.

Clarence wanted to stop by Mary's apartment to pick up some working gloves that he had left the day before, before going to his apartment. As we approached the apartment, I asked had he called Mary and told him that he was on the way. Mary was a nurse and worked the midnight shift. She normally is asleep during this time. Clarence said it is no problem in that he has a key and Mary is a deep sleeper.

At Mary's apartment, Clarence opens the door with his key but the door chain is on. This wasn't unusual, but when I looked inside the apartment I saw a bottle of vodka on the coffee table and two cups. Clarence drank rum not vodka. Furthermore, Isaac Hayes was playing. I stand accused. My mind started wondering and fearing for the worst. I told Clarence, "Let's go. Mary must be in a deep sleep and we shouldn't disturb her."

Clarence said, "The hell with that!" and broke the door in. It was a very loud noise. The dead could have heard that sound. Clarence immediately ran to the bedroom with me close behind. In the bedroom, we saw what I suspected. Mary was in the bed with another man, having sex.

Mary saw us and attempted to tell her partner that someone was in the room, but her partner was heavily involved in the sex act.

It wasn't until Clarence started yelling that Mary's partner realized we were in the room. When the man turned his head and look at us, I couldn't believe my eyes. It was Tommy, another police officer that worked with us in our police squad.

Clarence pulled his weapon and pointed it at Mary and Tommy. I grabbed Clarence and disarmed him, removed the bullets from the weapon, and threw them out the window. Today, I don't know why I did that. I just knew I wasn't going to lose my government job or go to jail because of a stupid act by others.

Mary jumped out of the bed and ran into the bathroom. I yelled at Tommy and told him to get the hell out of the apartment. Tommy grabbed his clothes, including his firearm, and ran out the front door with no clothes on.

Clarence started cursing Mary, calling her every bad name in the book. I forced my friend out of the apartment as I was younger and stronger then him. Clarence started to cry as we get into my vehicle and continued to curse Mary.

We go to my apartment and started drinking. We drank almost a whole half gallon of rum and got very drunk. Clarence stated that he was going to leave Mary and find another girlfriend. A few hours later, we both fall asleep and went to work the next day. Clarence made me promise that I will not tell anyone about the incident. I told Clarence that he was my friend and I would never do anything that would hurt him. He thanked me and said that he was lucky to have a good friend as me in his life. Tommy called in sick the next day and requested a transfer to another police district which was approved.

For the next two weeks, Clarence stayed at my apartment. We never mentioned Mary, but I could tell that he was very upset. He really loved Mary and wanted to marry her.

At the end of the two weeks, Clarence said he was "ok" and was going back to his apartment and "get his life back together."

For the next two months, Clarence was very cold to me. He wouldn't talk much or return my phone calls. At work, he wouldn't even work with me. I said to myself, *Clarence is just working through the problem with Mary.* I knew he missed her very much.

During this time, Tommy attempted to explain to me what happened and thanked me for not allowing Clarence to hurt him. I told Tommy it wasn't my concern. I was just concerned about my friend, Clarence, and wanted him to be OK. Mary even called and attempted to explain, but I didn't entertain the conversation. I was attempting to contain the after-shocks.

Three police officers were involved and I didn't want anyone to lose their job or go to jail for doing something brainless. I have seen so many police officers do stupid things when it came to women, and I wasn't going to be part of that scenario.

Two months passed and Clarence still wasn't talking to me. I reported to work on a Monday and I learned that Clarence had transferred to another police district; not the same one that Tommy worked at. He even changed his phone number and apartment. I was dumfounded. I couldn't understand why my friend was acting the way he was. I knew that he was hurt, but after five years working together I felt I knew him. This was totally out of character for Clarence.

Furthermore, I was told that Clarence and Mary had gotten married over the weekend. This didn't shock me in that I knew Clarence was in love with Mary. If he could forgive her, then that was okay with me. I figured after a few months my friend would get himself together and give me a call. Those months turned into years.

The next thirty years, Mary and Clarence had three children and nine grandchildren. During that time, we never spoke or visited one another.

It really hurt me the first three years in that I thought we were friends and we really cared for one another. I guess I was wrong.

Even now, I remember the fun times that we had together as friends. I recall two 17-year-old young men joining the police department and having so many dreams and ambitions. I guess my being there on the day of the incident was too much for Clarence.

Clarence and Mary both retired and relocated to South Carolina in 1997. I wish my friend and his wife the best in their retirement.

Tommy married a 23-year-old police officer, at the age of 50. His wife left him the next year for another man.

The Construction Worker
1976
Chapter 16

It was approximately 5p.m. and I was patrolling on my police scooter in the 2700 block of Martin Luther King Avenue, Southeast. I received an assignment for a patron refusing to pay his bar tab. The 2700 block of Martin Luther King Avenue S.E., is known for its bars and dancing girls. It was happy hour and mostly construction workers attended the bars during this time. Drinks were half price.

I knew the bar very well. It was called the Crazy Girl and well known for the dancing girls and cheap drinks. They didn't have many problems there, just a few fights. I and another scooter unit were given the assignment, but being young and inexperienced, I didn't wait for my back up.

I walked into the bar and the place was crowded with girls dancing everywhere. It was a special day, all drinks were $1.00. The bouncer approached me and pointed the guy out to me and stated that he refused to pay for his drinks. Even though I had only 14 months on the job, I knew that I didn't want to talk to the subject while in the bar. This would give him a stage to perform on. I approached the subject, who was later identified as a Mr. Ron Banks.

I ask Mr. Banks to follow me outside. I said it very professionally and didn't talk down to the gentlemen. I didn't want him to think that I was trying to insult him, especially in front of his co-workers and the girls that were dancing.

Once outside, Mr. Banks appeared to be quiet upset. I knew I recognized him from somewhere, but I just couldn't put my finger on it. I asked why he refused to pay for his bar tab. It was only $7.00. It didn't make sense to get arrested for $7.00. Mr. Banks looks me right in my eyes and said, "I'm not going to pay for water-down drinks. I asked for Johnny Walker Blue Scotch and the bartender has been pouring cheap liquor and charging me an extra dollar for that cheap stuff."

I notice that Mr. Banks was in his fifties and built like a prize fighter. I didn't want to get him to upset. My back-up had not arrived; the help I should have waited for in the beginning. I also wasn't trying to disrespect the gentlemen. It was only $7.00 and not worth the headache. I was attempting to relay this to Mr. Banks, but he wasn't going to hear this.

I heard a loud noise and for a second I turn my head to the left. This is something that I shouldn't have done. You never take your eyes off people that you are talking with. This is called "Letting your guard down," and it will get you killed. For no apparent reason, Mr. Banks hit me in the face with his fist.

Being young, I refuse to go down. My head said, *stay up*, but my legs said, *we are going down*. I now knew what Muhammad Ali felt like when Joe Frazier hit him in the 13th round back in 1973, knocking him down to the canvass.

Just then, Officer Tommy Carter grabbed me from the back and said," I got you Kittrell."

Officer Griffin, who was Officer Carter's partner, ran towards Mr. Banks. Mr. Banks immediately threw his hands up saying, "I'm sorry. I don't want no problems. I didn't mean to hit that officer."

Officers Carter and Griffin were assigned to Wagon 191. When I was originally given the assignment, they responded to back me up. A good wagon crew will always be on the scene, if an arrest might have occurred. This way, the officers don't have long to wait for assistance. In this case, I was glad they responded.

The officers placed handcuffs on Mr. Banks and we transported him to the police district for processing. My face was hurting like I just had a tooth pulled without any medication. The officers said I should have my face looked at by a doctor. Being young, I said I was okay, but I wasn't.

When we arrived at the police district, Mr. Banks started crying and said "Officer Kittrell, I am so sorry. I didn't mean to hit you. I was just upset. My wife left me this morning. She even had the boyfriend pick her up at the house. Now you know that takes a lot of balls. My wife is 30 and I am 59. I know the age is a little different, but I thought it would be okay.

"I met my wife 9 months ago and I fell in love right then. I knew she was a dancer, but she appeared to be a nice girl; no kids, takes care of her mother back in Georgia, didn't even use bad words, never. She didn't smoke or drink liquor and went to church every Sunday. I thought I had a nice girl."

When he told me that, I looked at him right in the face and said, "But, she was shaking her stuff every night for money with no clothes on."

Mr. Carter replied, "Officer Kittrell, that doesn't mean she isn't a good girl."

I just stop talking and said to myself, *I hope the judge gives you life for being stupid.*

I asked Mr. Banks what was his wife's name. He said, "Louise, but her stage name is Kitty Cat."

I stop writing and looked at him. "Mr. Banks does your wife wear a cat suit during her performance?"

"Yes, the guys really like it."

I knew that because, the police had hired her for a bachelor's party last Saturday and some guy dropped her off at the party. Then I remembered it was Mr. Carter that had dropped the dancer off and came back in three hours to pick her up.

Kitty Cat had put on a good show and the guys paid her extra money for doing such a good job. Now she was a performer and there was only one girl and 30 policemen. I ask Mr. Banks, "How in the hell can you allow your wife to dance for a living and guys putting their hands all over her like she was the only girl in the world."

"Well, officer, when I first met my wife she was dancer and made good money. She came home every night and I have never had a woman love me the way that women could."

I asked Mr. Banks, "Why in the hell did you hit me?"

"Officer Kittrell, I am so sorry and I am not a violent man. I make good money. My wife left me today for another man and it was a policeman that picked her up and drove my wife out of my life. I am so sorry. I will pay for all damages and do my time in jail. Also, that punk looks something like you; just a little."

Mr. Banks made bail and left the police station. I did go to the doctor and had my injuries attended too.

Three weeks later, I attended another police bachelor's party and guess who the entertainment? Kitty Cat! The police officer that she was living with drove her to the party. Three hours later he picked her up and drove away. I couldn't believe it.

Kitty Cat and the police officer got married and she continued to dance for a few years. Police parties where her specialty. She even gave them a discount for the performance. When I retired in 1995, Kitty Cat and the officer were still married.

What the hell!

My First Suicide
1976
Chapter 17

"I have lost my son and to lose a son is to lose a soul."
LT Marco F. Kittrell, MPDC, (ret)

As a young man growing-up in Washington, DC, I really enjoyed my childhood. It was a beautiful place to live. People, at that time, were always looking after you. It appeared that wherever I went everyone knew my parents or someone in my family. I really enjoyed the city and what it had to offer.

I was never exposed to the evils of the world. My parents always protected me and I had great grandparents, uncles, and aunts. I even knew my great grandparents. My entire family attended the same church, 10TH Street Baptist Church, located in Northwest Washington, DC.

At the time, I didn't appreciate what I had. I would walk through the church and see my family members all through the church. I assumed that was normal for everyone. How wrong I was.

On Saturday nights, I would watch cowboy movies with my grandfather until 12 midnight. In those days, the television would go off at 12 midnight. As a child, I assumed the world ended at 12 midnight. My childhood was a sense of safety and sometimes I wish I could go back to those days. It has been said that as a child you acted like a child and when I became a man I put away childish things.

My upbringing dictated my morals and even attitude towards people. As a police officer, they would change somewhat, but not to the point of changing my value system. During my career, I would be subjected to some of the cruelest and most outrageous acts by men and women that a person could imagine. I learned very soon that the world is a cruel place and mean people live in our world. This doesn't mean that you must succumb to such evils. You don't need to be a product of your environment, especially if you work in such a negative atmosphere.

There were times that if I was working and the job started getting to me, I would drive to a school and watch children play, chase each other, throw balls, and play on the swing bars. This gave me a comfort and strengthened my belief in that there were good people in the world and God had a plan for all of us. If the schools were closed, I would drive through the better neighborhoods and watch people cut their grass, cook on the grills, and wash their cars or see children play with their mother and fathers. This was a big lift for me as it reminded me of my family.

On one occasion, I received a radio assignment to respond to 1300 Congress Place, S.E. for the unconscious subject. It was approximately 8:00 a.m. On my arrival, I observed several people standing in front of the house. Some of them were on the ground holding each other. I said to myself, *this is going to be a bad one.*

Before I could exit my vehicle, this little girl ran over to my police cruiser, crying and yelling," My brother is dead! My brother is dead!"

The little girl's name was Tammy and she was 11 years old. I looked at this child, thinking, *where are all the adults?*

I exited my vehicle, took Tammy into my arms, and said, "Baby everything is going to be ok. Where are your parents?"

She looks down to the ground and said, "I don't know," and continued crying.

Another woman ran out of the house and yelled, "Officer, come in quickly."

Tammy called to the women, saying, "Aunt Helen why did my brother shoot himself." The women grabbed Tammy and the child held on to her aunt as if she was about to fall off a 10-story building.

By this time several other police officers had arrived on scene and we enter the house. One officer stayed outside and attempted to take control of the situation. Once inside, I saw more people crying and yelling at each other, accusing one another of the young man's death.

I saw a middle age woman, who was later identified as Ms. Jane, sitting in a chair. It appeared that she is in shock. I approached Ms. Jane and asked, "Are you ok?"

Ms. Jane lifted her head up, looked me in my eyes, and said, "My son is dead. I can't understand why my 16-year-old son would shoot himself."

By this time, the detectives and ambulance crew had arrived. I asked Ms. Jane, "Where is your son?" and told her we would take care of him.

Ms. Jane started crying and said, "My son is in his bedroom upstairs. I'll take you up to him."

I told Ms. Jane we would handle it and take good care of her son. Two officers stayed down stairs with the family while Officer Frank Curtis and I walked upstairs into the bedroom.

It was a site that I never forgot. As I walked into the room, I saw a young man on the bed covered in blood. He was later identified as Michael Jane.

Half of his head had been completed blown off. A shot gun was lying on the floor, smoke still coming from the barrel.

My First Suicide Case 1976

There was a large amount of blood and brain matter on the walls, which is normal when a person shoots their self in the head with a large weapon, close to a wall.

Officer Curtis said, "Why in God's name a boy would kill himself in such a way? It just doesn't make no damn reason why."

We interviewed the witnesses and satisfied ourselves that it was a suicide and not a homicide. All the evidence indicated the same. We later learned that Michael had broken up with his girlfriend and he couldn't handle the rejection. Michael had stolen the shotgun from his grandfather's home the day before.

On the day of the shooting, Michael entered his home and kissed his mother as she was cooking in the kitchen. He told his brother and sister that he loved them, as they are watching television in the living room. Michael walked upstairs and into his bedroom, where he had apparently hidden the weapon. Ms. Jane had felt a chill when her son kissed her and went upstairs to check on him. Seeing that everything was okay, she went back downstairs. Michael sat on his bed, placed the shotgun in his mouth, and pulled the trigger. After the weapon went off, Michaels' mother ran into the bedroom and saw her son lying on the bed.

Crying profusely, she stated, "I wish I would have stayed."

After the ambulance crew removed Michael's body, I looked around his room and all I could see were signs of a happy child's life. There were sports trophies, school books, pictures of his family members, and baby pictures. Everything a young man would want to have in his room - television, radio, record player, and two closets full of clothes - was there. Then I said to myself, *why would a young man kill himself in such a cruel way?* I just couldn't understand it.

I was well trained by the police department. In my short tenure, I had responded to many suicides as the assisting officer, arriving on the scene after the body had been removed and assisting with interviews and other secondary duties.

This was my very first suicide case where I was the leading officer and a child was involved.

Mr. Jane arrived home. He was unaware of his sons' death. He had been working his second job, driving a taxi. During those days cell phones and beepers did not exist. Mr. Jane walked into the house and asked his wife, "What is going on?" and "Why are the police in his home?"

Ms. Jane walked over to her husband, grabbed his hand, started crying again, and said, "Our son is dead. He has shot himself." Mr. Jane started crying and held his wife. They both fell to the floor, saying how much they loved their son and asking, "Why would he do such a thing?" Mr. Jane's father arrived at the home and picked up his son and daughter-in-law up saying, "I am here for the both of you. We will get through this."

It was a very touching moment. I stayed at the house for another hour, doing my job and attempting to comfort the family, but I felt that I was in the way.

After leaving the house I drove to a restaurant and ate breakfast. I sat in the corner and watched people go by thinking *how lucky they were to be living*. I even said that *the Jane's were lucky to have each other, even though their son was dead.* To see a family comfort each other in the manner that they did reminded me of my family.

This was my first suicide of a child and it made me feel bad. I just couldn't understand the reason for a child taking their life. During those days, it was very unusual to see a child commit suicide. In my short tenure on the department, I have been on several scenes involving adults who have committed suicide, but not children. I had no idea what was awaiting me in the upcoming years concerning children and suicides.

This was only the beginning. The next two years suicides among young people - under 17 years old - became a regular event occurring at least every three months or sooner. During the next twenty years, suicides became a normal event, especially among young people. I felt I was the only one that noticed this trend. I would comment on these suicides, but no other person acknowledged that it was unusual. I started feeling that maybe it was me and it wasn't a problem.

A year later an article was written in the newspaper acknowledging an increase in children committing suicides in the United States. I had my proof. I mentioned the article to some of my fellow officers, but they still refused to acknowledge that suicides were a serious problem. They used to tease me and say, "Rookie, you don't know what you are talking about.

That news article is nothing more than a person trying to sell papers to the suckers who didn't know any better." You must understand that in those days, that was the thinking of policemen when it came to changes or anything new.

These events finally were recognized and the problem addressed not only in Washington, DC, but the country as well. States, churches, cities, and organizations initiated a great crusade to educate the public on the dangers of suicide among children.

It took several years for the country to catch up, but I felt good that we were finally doing something about the problem. Even now I feel that I was part of history. I was there at the beginning to see those events affect all of us. It still hurts.

Even now, at my age, I check on my children and now my grandchildren.

The Traffic Accident 1976 Chapter 18

It was approximately 5:30 p.m. and I had a call for a traffic accident with injuries on the Anacostia Freeway. It was rush hour and I could see that traffic was backed up on the freeway. The Anacostia Freeway is the main travel route for traffic in and out of Washington, DC, and it was Friday and a holiday weekend.

During that time on the police department, traffic control and enforcement was very important to the department. We processed approximately 1 million people daily as they made their way to and from the city. The department had a very large traffic enforcement branch that strictly addressed traffic issues, ranging from impounding vehicles, directing traffic and facilitating parades, demonstrations and the movement government personnel. This meant personnel in the District of Columbia and Federal Governments including congressmen, senators, foreign dignitaries and even the President of the United States.

It was the norm to receive phone calls from Congressman, Senators, Ambassadors, the Mayor's office and even the White House concerning traffic issues.

The department considered traffic control and enforcement one of its most important responsibilities. While in the police academy, a large portion of our training was geared towards traffic enforcement and regulations. If you received the right phone call from the wrong person concerning traffic issues, heads were going to roll. I have never seen police supervisors move so fast as when a traffic problem was reported and traffic was congested somewhere in the city. I have seen supervisors leave a homicide scene to handle a traffic problem. I have seen officers, sergeants, lieutenant, captains, even deputy chiefs, and commanders reassigned because of their lack of dedication to traffic issues. In other words, they screwed up.

Prior to the installment of a subway system in the city, the police department used to assign a traffic officer or a police cadet to traffic intersections throughout the city. Their main directive was to keep traffic moving at all cost. This assignment was from 7 a.m. to 9:30 a.m. and 4:00 p.m. to 7:30 p.m., Monday through Friday. The department had approximately 100 intersections covered.

Before I graduated from the police academy in 1975 I was a police cadet for three years, so traffic enforcement was already instilled in me and I knew what the deal was; Keep traffic rolling at all costs!

The Traffic Accident 1976

As I approached the traffic accident, I could see that everyone was standing around what appeared to be a body lying in the highway.

I exited my vehicle and was informed that an elderly lady had attempted to cross the highway during rush hour and was struck by a vehicle. An ambulance crew was already on the scene and they were attempting to perform CPR, but the lady had expired. I confirm the death, notified the dispatcher, and waited for the Traffic Division Officer to respond and conduct the investigation along with the coroner's office. Whenever an accident death occurs it is their responsibility to conduct the investigation, along with MPDC.

By this time traffic had gotten worse, but due to the circumstances, there wasn't much that I could do. I couldn't tamper with the accident, but the body was blocking one traffic lane. This left only one lane open, at a time when both lanes were needed to accommodate the flow of traffic.

People were also attempting to see what the problem was and, once seeing what appeared to be a body in the street, this only made things move much slower. We covered the body with a blanket, but this only made the accident more noticeable.

I was directing traffic and attempting to expedite the same when Sergeant Frank Warren arrives on the scene. The sergeant is a thirty-year veteran and a damn good sergeant.

He has taught me a lot about police work and he really enjoys his job. He likes being a policeman. The sergeant once told me that he wasn't going to retired until they made him.

The sergeant exited his vehicle as he is smoking his cigar, looked around at the traffic and said, "I be Got-Damned! Look at this damn shit! Traffic is back up to the Got-Damn White House! That will be one phone call that I will not be taking." He looked at me and started walking towards me, not taking his eyes off me.

"Kittrell, what the hell are you doing? Why is this traffic so fucked up?"

"Sergeant, I have an elderly woman that was struck by a vehicle and she was killed."

The sergeant looked at the deceased and said what only a thirty-year veteran can say. Kittrell, this woman is dead, and nothing we can do about it. She is dead. Move that bitch to the side and get my traffic rolling. Put another blanket over her, put two traffic cones around the body, and get my Friday, rush-hour, holiday weekend traffic moving now. Do you read me, Officer Kittrell?"

I said, "Yes, Sir!" I asked the two ambulance drivers to help me move the body - which they did - placed another blanket over the body, and place two traffic cones around the same.

The sergeant got back into his police cruiser, drove by me and said, "Keep my traffic moving, officer. What the hell is wrong with you? Over some damn dead body!"

The traffic immediately picked up. People started blowing their horns as they drove by me. Some even gave me the finger and I was called several unpleasant names.

The traffic officers arrived, they processed the scene, and the deceased was transported to the morgue. No one was charge in the incident.

The elderly lady was later identified as a homeless person that lived close to the expressway and just made a bad decision that day.

Once I completed my assignment, I stayed on the scene and just watched the traffic go by. It made me feel good for some reason to see traffic flowing well. I started thinking and I remembered my first traffic crossing in 1972. It was Monday morning at 7:30 p.m. and I was at Pennsylvania and 14th street, one block from the White House.

Traffic was backed up and I felt I was doing the best job that I could do. My intersection was at the end of the Pennsylvania Corridor and as I looked to my left, all I could see was police cadets in every intersection. Approximately twelve, doing the same thing that I was attempting to do; move traffic.

It was at that time when this young lady stuck her head out the window and said, "Boy, You got traffic backed up for 30 blocks. Get this traffic moving!"

Well, as a police officer I wasn't going to take that kind of disrespect from nobody. I turned my head to confront the young lady and to my surprise it was my mother. I said, "Mom, you can't yell at me while I am in uniform. It looks bad."

My mother replied, "Boy, you made me late for work. Get this traffic moving! Love you and bye."

My father who was driving just looked at me and said nothing. He just shook his head and smiled. The other cars drove by and everyone said, "Boy, Get this traffic moving," and laughed. It wasn't my best day as a police officer.

As the sun went down, I said a prayer for the deceased and wonder if the traffic officers would be able to locate her family.

I also thought about Sergeant Warren's comments. I didn't like the way he talked about the deceased, but he represented his era and their thinking. The sergeant was correct in that traffic must flow or bigger problems will occur. I also liked the sergeant because he was a good man and really cared about people. I had seen him too many times make decisions that reflected his true feelings concerning people.

The sergeant worked after 35 years as a policeman. He died two years after he retired. I attended the funeral. He was a good man and supervisor. Great job, Sergeant Warren.

A Man in Love

1977

Chapter 19

"I loved thee and I killed thee because thee loved me and killed me"
LT Marco F. Kittrell, MPDC, (ret)

It was 7:30 p.m. and we were busy. I was receiving run after run. I couldn't wait until 11:30 p.m. when I got off the clock. It was Friday and I had something to do. One of the officers in the other shift was having a party and I knew everybody was going to be there. I was 22 years old and was trying to do everything at 22.

It was at that time Officer Wallace King and I received a radio assignment for a woman shot. I immediately responded to the scene with the red lights and siren blasting. I loved that stuff. It was fun, but serious. I was just like any other young police officer. If you every meet a police officer and they were 22 years old at any time during their career and they tell you anything different, they are lying. It is a rush that you can only appreciate once you have experienced the thrill of everyone moving out your way and looking at you as the world has stopped. It is on you, one big rush.

I arrived on the scene and I saw a large crowd surrounding, what appeared to be a young woman who wasn't moving.

The ambulance crew arrived right behind me and immediately started to go to work. They were good at what they do. I used to love to see those young people work, especially on people that had been seriously injured. The ambulance crew had a little God complex working too. They had their own rush going on when dealing with life and death situations, but they were good.

There was this young fireman named, Mary Wilson and she could have been a doctor. Mary could work on anybody and anything, the more blood the better. The doctors at the hospital loved Mary, but also hated her. They thought that she spent too much time with their patients attending to their injuries on the street. Mary didn't care. She knew what she was doing. Like I said *a little God complex*.

Mary said to me that the victim had been shot with what appeared to be a shotgun and immediately went to work on the person.

Several witnesses told me what happen. The victim, who was later identified as Helen Childs, 24 years old, had exited her vehicle and was in the process of walking into her apartment when a white Cadillac pulled up. An older gentleman exited the vehicle, produced what they recognized as a sawed-off shot gun, and pointed the same at Helen. He yelled, "Bitch, this is the last time that you will cheat on me!" and fired two rounds at Helen, striking her in the chest and stomach. The suspect then walked over to Helen and said, "Bitch, die slowly." Then he threw the shotgun in the back seat of his vehicle, drove off in the Cadillac, very slowly, looking back at Helen in his rear-view window. It appeared that the suspect was laughing.

One of the witnesses said that Helen was a fast-living young woman who had many men visiting her always of the day. They thought that she was a prostitute. But, Helen attended church every Sunday. Another witness said that, "Even prostitutes need the lord."

I said to myself, *another group of people passing judgment on other folks.*

A few minutes had passed, the crime scene was secured, and I had broadcast a lookout for the wanted vehicle and suspect. I asked Mary for an up-date on Helen, as the technicians were working to save her life. It looked like Mary was in her own world. Like I said, *the more blood, the more of a rush for Mary,* but she was damn good at her job.

I said. "Mary, if anything ever happens to me, I pray to God that you are on the scene attending to my wounds." Mary just looked at me and smiled and stated that they were about to transport Helen to the hospital.

After being shot with a sawed-off shotgun at close range, Helen was still holding on for dear life. As they put Helen into the ambulance, Mary looks at me and said, "I am God. I could have saved Jesus, himself." She winked her eye and I knew she was kidding, but I never knew anyone that loved their job as much as Mary.

It didn't take long for the detectives to get the name of the suspect. He was identified as Jimmy Walker. We had his home, and work address and everything that we needed to arrest him. One thing I loved about my job was working with the detectives. They were good and they always made you feel part of the team. It may seem minor, but I always liked when they called me by my first name, Marco. It made me feel like one of them. All I needed was a suit and a hat . . . also; I had to gain 40 pounds.

We would get in a circle and start talking about what, where, who, and why. I loved that stuff and I learned so much about police work in those discussions. That is what you don't see on television or at the movies, real work and professionals demonstrating their trade. Just damn good cops.

During those days, if someone was shot, stabbed, or killed on one day, they were arrested the next day. These guys were good, knew it, and demonstrated to everyone how it was done. As a 22 year-old police officer, I was like Mary; having a rush and enjoying every minute of it.

Forty minutes later a foot beat officer observed Jimmy's vehicle in the 2700 block of Martin Luther King Avenue. The detectives and I immediately drove to the scene and placed a stake out on the vehicle. A short time later Jimmy walked over to the vehicle and placed a bag into the trunk.

He then walked towards a club that was known as the Bee Hive. The establishment is well recognized in the community as a place for cheap drinks and fast woman. Police officers go there all the time when off duty, which is a violation of police rules, but only if they catch you.

The detectives put a plan in place, covered all the exits, and sent two undercover officers into the club to keep an eye on Jimmy. They said, "We have plenty of time. Let Jimmy have a few drinks. He might be easier to handle." They didn't want a gun battle. At the time that they had observed Jimmy at his vehicle, to many people were in the parking lot.

So, we are in the unmark police cruiser waiting for Jimmy to come out the club. The three detectives start talking about food. I am sitting in the back of the cruiser and all they talked about was what they were going to eat after they arrested Jimmy. They went from chicken to ribs to fast food. Then they started arguing about the damn food; about who was going to go get it, who was paying, and when they were going to get the food. I said to myself, *a woman is seriously shot, the suspect is sitting in a bar, and we are talking about damn food. Maybe that was the reason why I wasn't a detective; my priorities were out of order.*

Jimmy stayed in the club for approximately two hours, has several drinks, and then leaves. As soon as he approached his vehicle and attempted to put the key in the door lock, the detectives subdued him without incident. They walked right up to him and said, "Jimmy! Police! Don't move! We got you. Place your hands behind your back. No problems or we will kill you as you stand." Jimmy complied.

We transported Jimmy to the police district for processing. While at the district, Jimmy confess to the shooting and we recover the shotgun from the truck of Jimmy's car. As we interview Jimmy, he tells his story. By this time in my career, I knew what the story was.

Jimmy had been dating Helen for approximately 1 year, paying all the bills. He was in love. Jimmy was 60 years old and Helen was 24. She made him feel good in many ways. Helen had been cheating on him with other men and women, but Jimmy forgave her every time.

Three weeks ago, Helen had stolen money from Jimmy's checking account and took her new boyfriend on a 10-day cruise. Once Jimmy learned of the affair, he couldn't take it anymore and he decided to shoot Helen. It was a sad story, but he was in love.

As we continued the interview, the phone rang and we

learned that Helen had succumbed to her wounds. We told Jimmy that now he is facing a murder charge and the case will be handled by the homicide Unit. Jimmy started crying. The detective looked at each as if to say, *it is too late for that. You should have thought of that before you killed her.* But, they didn't say anything. They were pro's and didn't want to humiliate Jimmy. There was a code between criminals and detective, but that is another story.

Once Jimmy is transported to the Homicide Unit, the food finally arrived in the office. I asked, "When did you order the food?"

Immediately they said, "When we first reported to work at 3 p.m." It was 10 p.m., by this time.

I couldn't figure it out. I asked, "Why in the hell were they arguing about the damn food earlier?" They just looked at me and started laughing.

I asked if I could partake of the feast and one of the detectives said, "Why should you? You didn't contribute anything to the meal."

Another detective stated, "Neither did we. Let's eat." Everything that they had argued about was in the office. I could see why they were all 30 pounds overweight.

The next day I saw Mary and said I was sorry that Helen had died. Mary said, "Don't sweat it. I did my job, it was those damn doctors. Besides, two shots to the stomach and chest by a shotgun as close range? I was amazed that she made it to the hospital. Oh yea, I worked on her."

Mary and I would work on many cases during the next three years. We really became good friends. Mary married another police officer and they are still together today.

Jimmy pled to second degree murder and was sentenced to 25 years to life. Washington, DC, doesn't have the death sentence.

The detectives that I had worked with on that case all retired and are doing well. They have a reunion every year, at a restaurant, all you can eat, and are still 30 pounds' overweight.

Mr. Johnson
1977
Chapter 20

I received a radio assignment for a man shot at 1955 Shipley Terrance Southeast. On my arrival, I saw a very large crowd surrounding a young man, a teenager lying on the ground. The ambulance crew had arrived and they were attending to his wounds. The young man had been shot in the buttocks.

As I exited my vehicle, several people approached me and said that a man named, Mr. Johnson, had shot the young man. They pointed where Mr. Johnson lived.

By this time, my partner, Officer John Wallace, arrived on the scene. I briefed him and we walked towards Mr. Johnson's home, which was located right in front of the shooting scene. Mr. Johnson identified himself as Mr. Michael Johnson.

Mr. Johnson was sitting in a rocking chair reading a paper. As we approached, we saw a large amount of smoke on the porch and it smelled like gun powered. Therefore, I assumed he must have use a revolver as they give off more smoke than other firearms. I walked up to Mr. Johnson and asked if he knew anything about the shooting of the young man, later identified as David.

Mr. Johnson said, "No. Somebody probably shot this young punk ass because he refuses to stop sitting on somebody's car."

I said, "Mr. Johnson, several people identified you as the person that shot the young man and I see and smell all this gun smoke on your porch, which gives me evidence that you are the shooter."

Mr. Johnson replied, "Officer, I am 89 years old and I am no liar. I shot the young punk. I told him to stop sitting on my brand-new Cadillac."

"He told me to, 'Kiss his ass.'"

"I said, "Ok, be here when I get back." I went to my bedroom and got my pistol and returned. The little punk was still sitting on my brand-new Cadillac."

"He said' "Old man, what the hell do you want now? You better get going before you get hurt."

"He turned his back to me and shoved his ass into my face and said, "Kiss my ass." I removed my pistol and shot him twice in the ass. I then walked back to my porch and finished reading my paper. That will be the last time that punk will sit on someone's car again and tell them to "Kiss his ass."

I asked Mr. Johnson, "Where is the pistol that you used to shoot the young man?"

Mr. Johnson told me to look in his bedroom under the bed. I went to the bedroom and, after looking under the bed, I found not one, but 30 pistols.

I approached Mr. Johnson and inquired into his arsenal of weapons. Mr. Johnson stated that he had been collecting weapons for approximately 70 years and they were his property. He told me to take the one that he used and he was ready to go. I informed Mr. Johnson that I was going to take all the weapons and he was facing some serious charges.

Mr. Johnson made a phone call and his lawyer met us at the police district. The lawyer was one of best in the area and I knew him well. All the police officers respected him and were afraid of his abilities. He was a good lawyer.

During the trial, the prosecutor and his lawyer worked out a deal and Mr. Johnson received probation. The judge and the prosecutor knew Mr. Johnson. I didn't know at the time that Mr. Johnson was a retired professor of law. He had been teaching and practicing law for over 60 years throughout the United States. The young man that was shot survived his injuries and refused to testify in court.

After the trial, I started stopping by Mr. Johnson's home once a week and talking with him. He was a very interesting person to speak with. I loved history and Mr. Johnson trained and educated me a about black history, especially Washington, DC.

When I walked thru his home, I was so amazed to see all the beautiful items that he had, especially the pictures and paintings that he had collected over the years from around the world. Mr. Johnson had a very fulfilling life, from my point of view. He had visit countries like China, Russia, Egypt, Cambodia, and Japan. He even spoke three different languages.

Mr. Johnson had five children, twenty-five grandchildren and ten great grandchildren. They all cared about him and always were visiting and calling on him. His wife, Mary, had died before his purchase of the Cadillac and he missed her very much. He was always talking about her and constantly said how much he loved his wife. The reason that he lost his control with the young man that he had shot, right or wrong, was that he had purchased the Cadillac for his wife and she died the day that he had purchased the vehicle.

By the young man sitting on the vehicle and being so disrespectful, Mr. Johnson considered the young man being disrespectful to his Wife, even though she had died and wasn't there.

I loved talking with Mr. Johnson. He was some gentlemen and from a good family. He loved being old, because he still wanted to teach and educate people.

Mr. Johnson really regretted shooting David, because as

an educator and sensible man he should have been able to talk with him. His emotion got the best of him and he could only think about his lovely wife. Mr. Johnson further stated that he had asked God for forgiveness for committing such a terrible sin.

Mr. Johnson further told me that he had paid David's doctor bills and offered compensation to his family. David's father refused the money and said that his son was wrong for being so disrespectful, but he still didn't want his child shot. Mr. Johnson and David's family have been attending church every Sunday for the past few months, attempting to heal the incident.

Mr. Johnson contacted several of his friends in the school system and got David a full scholarship to his college, Howard University. David attended college and graduated four years later. Mr. Johnson was there.

During Mr. Johnson's and David relationship, David met Mr. Johnson's granddaughter, Mary, and they later married after they graduated from college. Mary attended Hampton University. Virginia. Mr. Johnson was also at the wedding.

Mr. Johnson died the same year of the wedding, approximately two months later. It was the biggest funeral that I have ever observed. David cried the most.

Mr. Johnson was 94 years old at the time of his death.

In Mr. Johnson's will, he left David and Mary his house and the Cadillac. The Cadillac had very few miles. David drove the vehicle, to his High School prom, college graduation ceremonies and his wedding. David had the license plates change to read, "Mary."

In 1995, David still had the Cadillac. He and Mary had three children. Their first child was a boy and he was named Michael after his great grandfather. Their second child was a girl and she was name Mary after her great grandmother.

I miss Mr. Johnson. He was a good man. I just wish he would have sold me the Cadillac.

Detective John Smith
1977
Chapter 21

It was Monday evening and Mike Champ and I were working together. At approximately 4:30 p.m. we received a radio assignment for the sounds of gun fire in the 4600 block of Martin Luther King Avenue. We immediately acknowledged the dispatcher and responded.

On our arrival, we observed several people standing in front of the apartment building. Several people ran over to our vehicle and started telling us that a young man had been shot and he was lying in a pool of blood in the basement laundry room. We advised the dispatcher and requested an ambulance and additional backup.

Officer Champ and I ran towards the basement with our guns drawn. Immediately after entering the laundry room we saw a young man lying on the floor face down. It appeared that he had been shot in the head. He wasn't moving. I smelled the gun smoke and started thinking, *where was the suspect and was he or they still in the area?* Officer Champ advised the dispatcher and requested the assistance of a detective unit and the estimated time of arrival of the ambulance.

I checked for signs of life as Officer Champs was pointing his weapon in all directions believing that the suspect could be in the immediately area. I turn the body, face towards me, to administered CPR. To my surprise, I recognize the young man.

I said, "Champ," in a very soft voice, "It is Detective John Smith." Detective Smith was assigned to the Vice Unit. Officer

Champ replied, "Damn it! What in the hell is he doing here?" I informed the dispatcher that the man shot is a police officer.

I didn't tell the officer's name over the police radio. This was because the press monitored the police channel and you always wanted to tell the officer's family first when there is a serious injury, especially when death was involved. I administered CPR, but I could tell that the detective was dead. I just had to do something. While administering CPR, Detective's Smith eyes are wide open and it appears that he is looking at me. This was the first time that I have ever been on the scene of an officer that was shot.

I am saying to myself and praying to God that the detective will make it, but the signs were not good.

The ambulance crew finally arrived and took over. I

could tell once they checked the vital signs, they knew that the officer was dead and he was gone.

Other officers arrived and we all started canvassing the area for witnesses. Within minutes, we learned what happen and established a suspect. The witness told us that they had seen the young man in the building on many occasions in the past two weeks. We did not tell them the identity of the Detective Smith.

The witness further told us that the young man has been in the company of a suspect named James and we further identify James' address. It was now we learned that Detective Smith had died. We were all taken back by the death but we continued working. It is different, when a police officer dies, you know their family and it hurts.

Once we located James' apartment, the detectives knocked on the door as my partner and I stand adjacent to the door. The detectives yelled out, "Police open the door." James opened the doors and said, "Officers, please come in and have a seat." In a very pleasing voice James said, "I knew you officers would be here soon. I guess it is about the punk that tried to rob me down stairs in the basement. I knew I should have called the police, but I was just to upset about the whole incident."

Now, I am taken back by the comments, but the detectives were veteran officers and were already making eye contact with each other, giving signals. I used to love watching those guys work during times like this.

James asked us to have a seat. The detectives immediately say, "Sure," but my partner and I remained standing, watching James the whole time. The detectives asked if it was alright for the police officers to look around his apartment.

James immediately said, "Okay" and "Look around. There is no one here but me." We searched the apartment and the place is spotless. Nothing was out of place. I have never seen an apartment so clean. Everything in the apartment cost more than my salary.

The detectives aren't talking. They are letting James talk. James is seated in a big white fur chair with his legs folded, drinking water, and smoking a cigarette. He is wearing a white silk robe, two gold rings on each hand, four gold chains around his neck, a gold ear ring in each ear, and smelling like a French woman. James takes a hit from his cigarette and began telling us his story.

"Officers, I was minding my own fucking business. I have been living here for nineteen years. Hell, I own the building. Shit, I am not a broke nigger. I have things. I just like living in the apartment. Now, that punk down stairs that I shot approached me while I was downstairs washing my cloths and pulls a piece out. Can you believe such shit? On me, a fucking piece! Telling me to 'give it up.' I guess he was talking about money.

"I have been carrying a gun for thirty-five damn years, sometimes two. So, I told the fucker, 'Ok, don't shot me,' and

'Please don't shot me like a bitch.' He approached me with his guard down. I just turned around and shot that fucker right in his head. He yelled like a little bitch.

"I don't know why he picked me to rob. I guess he picked the wrong mother-fucker."

He started smiling as he smoked his cigarette. It was at that time James looked in all our faces and he stared. He could see that we didn't like the statement. "Wait a minute, was that fucker a policeman? I will be got-damn! The city isn't paying you guys enough money, that you are required to start robbing poor people like me to make ends me. Now that is a bitch!"

James pointed his finger at us as he continued to talk, "Now, I always felt that the police were under paid. Last year, when the city placed on the ballot the question to give you guys a pay raise, I said, 'Hell yes. Give the police a raise.' There are some dangerous mother-fuckers out there, which will cut your throat and piss on your grave. Officers, I support everything you guys do.

"You know last year when they attempted to raise money to buy the officers bullet proof vests, I donated $1,000 to the cause. Hell, the vest you are wearing, I probably paid for the same. Keep doing the good job that you police are doing officers. God save fucking America!"

James attempted to go into his pockets and we stopped him, even though I had already searched him and the chair that he was sitting in.

He said, "I am sorry officers. I know that you are probably jumpy, just after me killing your fellow police officer, but I just wanted to make another donation to any police cause that you may know."

"Hell, I have killed another police officer. Yes, sir. Another officer tried to rob me 10 years ago at 14Th and T Streets, N.W. I was in the alley, minding my own fucking business and that mother-fucker pulled a gun. I had to defend myself and I shot that mother-fucker in the head. Yes, sir. The police arrested me, like they should. America being the country that it is, they couldn't convict me on Murder-1, so I pleaded to Manslaughter. Did three years and got out. What the hell, only in America. You know, you police really get upset when a police officer dies in the line of duty. People start crying, flags are lowered, and the wife's get all that fucking money. He shakes his head. She probably starts fucking the next day, probably her husband's best friend. You police need to check yourselves, a lot of people don't like that kind of shit."

"Look at you guys. You look like someone just fucked your sister and you thought she was a virgin. Man, those bitches been fucking me for years."

He started laughing. We just listened. James had smoked three cigarettes by this time. He continued and told us that he had already called his lawyer and he was advised not to say anything. "But, I know my rights. I was in my rights to defend myself. That fucker tried to rob me. What a damn shame when a police officer goes bad."

Well officers, shouldn't you be reading me my rights or something? Do you want the firearm that I use to shoot that fucker with? It is right in my top dresser."

I retrieved the firearm and by this time James' lawyer had arrived. James jumped up and said, "This is my lawyer, Attorney Joe Weinberg. The best damn Jew white-boy lawyer in the world."

He throws his arm around the attorney. "Do you know how much money I pay this mother-fucker? A lot, I will tell you, but he is worth every dime. I am always getting in shit, not my fault.

The attorney told James to stop talking and have a seat and advised the detectives that his client would not make any more statements. The detectives told the attorney, "That is ok, but James must go to the police district for further investigation."

The attorney asks if his client is under arrest, the detectives respond, "That is right."

James is arrested and handcuffed by me.

As we walked out the door, James looked at all the policemen there on the scene. The police in turn stare at James with hate. James told me, "Now, you see that officer? They hate me but not that stealing, robbing, police bitch that crossed the line. You know what I mean? What a world we live in."

Once at the police district, the detectives continued their investigation. They told me later that they didn't want to stop James from talking. If he initiated the conversation, it was legal. I further learned that James was one of the biggest heroin dealers in the city.

Detective Smith was working on a case against James, but the detective was over his head and didn't follow proper police protocol concerning the case. He didn't keep his fellow officers advised of his whereabouts. He didn't tell them all that concerned the case.

On the day that he was killed, he had arranged with James to buy a kilo of drugs, but James got suspicious. He probably killed the detective, knowing that he was alone and not wired. During the trial, the evidence was weak, but we did get a conviction for Murder-Two. James stated that he was the victim of a robbery attempt by Detective Smith, but the jury didn't buy his story. James was sentence to twenty-five years; too many holes in his story. When the jury came back with their verdict, James told the jury, "Fuck you all!"

I learned a lot during the investigation like how to investigate people and let their own weaknesses and strengths kill them. It was sad that Detective Smith was killed, but I learned from his death. I learned to never go it alone when working undercover; you always need back-up.

It was later learned in the investigation that James had infiltrated the vice office and had turned Detective Wells. The detective was working for James and gave him a lot of information concerning drug cases in the area. We could never prove that James was given information concerning Detective Smith.

Detective Wells in question was later discovered during a sting operation that was conducted by the FBI.

We all wanted to connect him to Detective Smith murder, but we couldn't. Detective Wells was convicted of several felonies and sentenced to 30 years in prison for his crimes.

I always felt that Detective Smith knew more about Detective Wells and just didn't want to turn him in. They had been partners two years earlier. Both cases left several holes that were never filled. It stills hurts.

The Little People
1977
Chapter 22

"I might be short but you are shorter"
Lt. Marco F. Kittrell, MPDC retired

I received a radio assignment for the fight at 121 Danbury Street, Apartment #4, Southeast. I knew the area. It is a very quiet area and normally didn't receive radio assignments. I should have waited for my back-up, but being young and believing that it was a milk run, an easy assignment, I responded without waiting for another police officer. These types of radio runs are normally handled by two police officers. I should have waited for my partner.

I walk into the apartment building and I hear this commotion coming from apartment #4. I knock on the door and when the door opened I see this little female midget. I started to stare. I didn't mean to stare but I have never seen a midget up close. The women immediately told me that her husband had been beating on her and she was very concerned for her safety. The women identified herself as Mary and her husband's name was Bill.

I ask, "Where is Bill?"

Mary calls for her husband, "Bill, this police officer wants to see you right now."

As I look around the apartment, Bill emerges from the kitchen and he is another midget. I started laughing. I was only 21 years old. I wasn't attempting to disrespect Bill, I was just young.

Bill walks over to me, "Who in the fuck are you laughing at, Bitch?"

I was not going to allow a midget to outdo me, so I told Bill that it wasn't necessary to curse at me and let us talk about the situation. Bill takes two steps back into the apartment.

"Fuck you, bitch. I will place my foot in your ass." Bill calls out in a very loud voice, "John! Tate! Carry!"

Three more midgets ran into the room, I responded "Wow, the circus must be in town."

Bill says, "Bitch, you got jokes. Rush this tall fucker and kick his ass."

I said, "Rush who? No midget going to hang foot in my ass."

The Little People 1977

That was the beginning of my down fall. Bill was the first to hit me. He kicks me in the left leg, causing me to fall. Bill and the other midgets jumped on me. Tate bites me on my arm. I bite Tate on his ear.

Tate says, "That bitch bit me on my ear."

We continue to fight and the midgets begin dragging me towards the window, kicking me along the way.

Bill told the other midgets, "Pick this bitch up and throw him out the window."

As they are attempting to throw me out the window, I began kicking with my boots and hitting them with my police baton, with no effect. I was not going to allow these little people to win the battle.

At the time, I was unaware that midgets were so strong.

But, I was young and determined to win the battle. I hit Bill in the eye and the other midgets in the face with my baton. I finally get to my police radio and called for help.

My back up arrived very quickly and we arrested everyone in the house, including Mary. During the fight, Mary joins in the assault and threw beer bottles at me, striking me several times.

My fellow police officers considered the incident very funny and felt that I should have been able to handle the midgets. They all made fun of me by saying,

"Kittrell, didn't you know that the circus was in town?"

"Kittrell, didn't you take the midget defense course while in the police academy?"

"Kittrell, you didn't know that midgets were known to kick police officers ass and take names?"

"Kittrell, the midgets said if they had another three minutes, your ass would have been theirs."

"Kittrell, the midgets said this fight is not over and they will see you again."

Kittrell, the midgets are calling their big brother to kick your ass, he is three feet tall."

"Kittrell, the midgets said after they pay their bail, they are coming after your ass."

"Kittrell, the midgets ask how much it costs to kick a police officer's ass in this town because they have plenty of money."

"Kittrell, the midgets said you fight like a bitch."

The comments were not the thing that I wanted to hear, but that was the police way and I knew that I would never live this down. After an hour, I started laughing myself, but my troubles had just started.

The midgets were charged with Assault on a Police Officer, which is a felony in Washington, DC, and denied bail.

That meant that they would appear in court the next day after spending the night in jail. If I knew what was going to happen the next day, I would have set those midgets free that day if I could. My agony had just begun.

I arrived in court that Saturday morning. My arm is in a sling with a minor fracture. I'm missing two teeth, my left leg is very sore, and I'm walking with a very bad limp and using a walking cane. It wasn't my best moment, but I was determined to see justice done

As I am walking into the court house, everyone in the police department has heard of my case with the midgets. Every police officer that walks by me, starts laughing. It made me feel very small. Some officers even made jokes, "Kittrell, watch yourself. I have seen some midgets walking around in the court house asking for you. They said something about 'throwing you out a window.'"

I said, "Very funny. Go find some police work, if you can, mother."

It was just police officers taking advantage of the moment. I knew how police officers could be when given the opportunity to make fun of something. I even laughed to myself.

When I entered the front door of the court house, I was greeted by Sergeant Thomas Smith. He was a thirty-year veteran of the force and I respected him very much. He looked at me and said, "Damn, Kittrell! Then he shook his head and walked out the door. Sergeant Smith is another story, I will tell you later.

On Saturday you are normally in and out of the court house very fast because everyone wants to go home. Normally the court house is closed by 12 noon. Not this day! My case was going before Judge James Jackson and he was aware of the case and wanted to have fun with me.

Judge Jackson made my case the last case on the docket for that day. He wanted to enjoy his Saturday with me. I knew the Judge and respected him as a judge, but he liked jokes and really enjoyed funny cases. He should have written a book.

My case is called. I walked into the court room, limping as I approach the bench. Judge Jackson immediately said, "Bring in those dangerous people who have assaulted one of my police officers. Officer Kittrell, you do not need to walk any further, have a seat where you are."

I said, "Yes, sir" and took my seat.

The court room was packed, not one seat was to be had. Then they bring in the four midgets and everyone just started laughing, even the Judge. Judge Jackson hits his gavel and calls for a recess.

During the hearing, the midgets are given bail. They plead guilty and are sentenced to 8 months, 2 years' probation, and fined $4000 each plus court cost.

It was one of my lowest moments as a police officer, but I learned from the incident and it made me a better police officer. I always told this story to many people. If you can't laugh at yourself then you will never grow as a person. Every police assignment that I had after the incident, I always waited for my back up. I attend Sergeant Smith's retirement ceremonies three years later and after the dinner he approached me and said, "Damn Kittrell" and walked away. I never saw those midgets' again.

Mary

1977

Chapter 23

"I love thee and I will be with thee until thee loves
me no more"
LT Marco F. Kittrell, MPDC, (ret)

I received a radio assignment for 2890 Alabama Avenue, SE to assist the ambulance crew with an unconscious baby. It was Monday at 9 a.m. I knew this area well, mostly inhabited by drug users.

On my arrival, I observed a fireman, who operated the ambulance, standing outside on the sidewalk crying. At that time I assumed that the child had died or was seriously injured. This was the first time that I had observed a fireman cry and it stunned me. I have seen many police officers and citizens cry, but no fireman. We all are human and Gods children.

As I approached the firemen, he looks at me and said, "How can people be so cruel, especially when dealing with children?"

He was very young and looked like he just completed high school. The fireman's name was John Jackson and had just graduated from the Fireman's Training Academy. I said to myself, *this is what we call on the police department as a person's baptisms under fire,* your first time dealing with a horrible situation.

I told John that everything would be okay and maybe he needs to stay outside for a while, but to deal with the situation, he would need to go back inside and do his job.

He said, "Ok, officer. You are right. I am ready to go back in."

As we walk into the apartment, I knew what to expect. The house was filthy with very little furniture and an odor that I have smelled before. All drug houses had that smell. There was even human waste on the floor.

I see a female fireman carrying a baby down the hallway with only a blanket around the baby. The baby appeared to be approximately 5 months old or younger. I learned later that the baby's name was Mary. The fireman looks as if she has seen a ghost. Another fireman takes the baby and said that the baby is dead. John walks back into the apartment and asks his supervisor was there anything else that he could do to help?

As I am about to start my investigation into the death of the child, a young lady walks into the apartment and introduced herself as the baby's mother. Her name was Karen. Karen looks like she has been up all night. Her hair looks like Don King's and smelled like a barn.

I could tell that she was coming down from a high; heroin use. I then recognized her as one of the prostitutes that worked in the area.

Karen asks why we are in her apartment and what is wrong with her baby. Karen walks over to the fireman that is carrying her child, looks at the baby, and started saying, "Wake up, Mary. Wake up!

Karen has a hard time standing. No one attempted to help Mary.

Karen further stated it is time to feed Mary. "She is always hungry. That is the problem. She just needs to eat something." Karen walks into the kitchen and opens the ice box. "Damn, no food. No wonder she is crying." Karen falls to the floor and starts laughing.

Everyone in the room has a look of disgust and wanted to just shake Karen until you shake the life out of her.

John runs over to her, picks Karen up and tells her that she was a terrible mother and she was the reason for her baby's death. The other fireman grabbed John and restrained him.

Karen replies, "Mister, you don't know the half of my story. I have been selling pussy for most of my life, used every drug under the sun, and did every bad thing that a person could possible think. I even stabbed a few mother-fuckers. They all deserved it. Well, it was this one bitch. I just didn't like the way she was looking at me, so I stabbed her in the chest. She didn't die, just bled and yelled like a pig. Then Karen started laughing.

The fireman escorted John outside and I grabbed Karen and placed her under arrest for cruelty to children. The detectives arrived and stated they would question her further and decide if they would charge her with homicide. I left the crime scene, drove for approximately two hours and I thought about Mary all day. No matter how long you may be a police officer, when dealing with children cases, they always hit home. You think about your children and how lucky you are for having children and they are home safe.

These types of cases make policemen very critical of people when they enter your immediately family circle. Not trusting people, especially your children friends, when they bring them home to meet the parents.

During the court trial, Karen was found guilty of cruelty to children. The prosecutor couldn't prove manslaughter, which was the lowest level of murder in Washington, DC. There are five different degrees of murder in Washington, DC.

One year later, I see Karen in an area that is frequent by prostitutes. I could tell that Karen was working again in that trade and she was pregnant. There were a lot of men who love to have sex with women that were pregnant, especially if the woman was a prostitute. I could never understand that.

I watch Karen for approximately one hour and she kept looking at me. Every few minutes she would leave the area and return. I notice and it appears that Karen had stop using drugs from my observation. She didn't have the signs of a drug user.

One month later, I drive by the area that I know Karen works. I see Karen, exit my vehicle and I walk up to her to inquire about her future. Before I could reach Karen, she surprises me and walks towards me. Karen asks how I was doing and if I had any children. This caught me totally off guard. Before I could respond, Karen further stated that she was sorry about Mary and she thinks about her daughter every day and that is her punishment from God. There are nights when she is unable to sleep and cries for Mary. I don't say anything because, all I can think about is that little baby that died because of Karen's failure to take care of her child.

Karen said goodbye and she hopes that I have a safe and good career. She walks a few feet away, stops, turns around and looks at me. "Officer Kittrell, I stopped using drugs. It is an everyday fight, but I am trying. I plan to stop doing this street thing very soon and move back home to Mississippi with my father. He doesn't know what I do and I plan to raise my child up-right. Pray for me."

I didn't say a word, because the job always surprises me when dealing with people.

The next few months I would drive by the avenue where Karen worked and I didn't see her. I checked the police reports and I didn't see Karen's name on any offense or arrest reports. I hope that she had relocated back home.

One year later, Karen sent me a post card with a picture of her and her new child. It was a little girl name Mary. They were in Mississippi living with her father on a far. She was working at a factory and she had met someone. She was doing fine. Karen stated she would do it right this time and asked me to forgive her for her past sins. She had been praying to God every night and she believed that God has forgiven her. I heard no more from Karen. I said a prayer for her and both Mary's.

John, the fireman, retired from the fire department the same year that I retired from the police department in 1995. He and his wife had one daughter and they named her Mary.

I always said that it wasn't for me to judge people. That was God's job and he is always watching.

South Capitol and Southern Avenue Southeast

1977

Chapter 24

"A day isn't promise but the end will always come".
LT Marco F. Kittrell, MPDC, (ret)

Two young men walked into a bank at 9:30 a.m., wearing masks, and produced hand guns and told the employees that this was a bank robbery and told everyone to hit the floor. There was one security guard standing at the front door and he was very old. Suspect #1, who was later identified as Jack, struck the guard to the face with his pistol, causing the guard to fall to the floor. He was knocked unconscious and almost died from the assault.

Suspect #2, who was later identified as Bill, jumped over the counter and told the employees, "If anyone sounds the alarm, I will kill them."

One of the employees, Karen, was 7 months pregnant and asked if she could lie on her back.

Bill said, "Hell no! I don't care about your baby or you," and threw Karen to the floor.

Bill began to remove the money from the casher's cage. It took only 2 minutes and the two suspects ran towards the front door. Before exiting, Jack kicked the security guard with his steel boot to the face, breaking the guard's nose.

Outside, the suspects attempted to get into their vehicle and make their escape. Officer Jake Wilson, driving a scooter, observed the suspects and radioed for assistance. Before the suspects reached their vehicle, Officer Wilson attempted to stop them. Both Jack and Bill fired several shots at Officer Wilson, none taking effect. The officer returned fire, missing both suspects.

A foot chase ensued. By this time, other police units had arrived and joined in the chase. Several more shots were exchanged by the police and the suspects. Bill was shot first, receiving two shots to the chest. He fell in the street. The money that he was carrying flew out the bag and spread over a four-block area.

Jack continued running, but was finally shot to the head as he ran by a police officer that just happened to be off-duty and in plain clothes. Jack was shot twice, falling and dying instantly. The money that he was carrying also came out the bag and flew in the wind for approximately six blocks. It took approximately four hours to recover the money, what was left over, approximately $4,500. It was reported that the suspects had stolen $15,000

By the time I arrived on the scene, it was all over. The whole incident from the armed robbery to the shooting of the suspects took only 10 minutes. Within that short time period, two young men died, a security guard was seriously injured and almost died from his injuries, and Karen, 23 years old, had a miscarriage losing her child. Karen, also, was unable to have any more children due to the injuries that she had received when Jack threw her to the floor.

It was a very sad day to see so many lives destroyed and damaged. Everyone woke up that morning believing they would return home the same way they had left for their jobs. Then Jack and Bill, two young men who had been in and out of jail for the last 10 years, decided to rob a bank. The result was Karen lost a child; a security guard was seriously injured and almost died from his injuries, and two police officers ending up killing two human beings.

Jack, 26 years old and Bill, 27 years old.

Officer Mark Shawn
1977
Chapter 25

Officer Mark Shawn was a very disturbed officer. He has been a police officer for approximately 9 years. This is a veteran police officer by Metropolitan Police Department standards. I had been working with Officer Shawn for approximately one year and I didn't like working with him. He was a terrible person when it came to understanding people and their problems.

As police officers, you usually deal with people who have committed crimes or hurt others (criminals), who have been hurt (victims), who are in adverse conditions. A result of dealing with mostly negative things is that some police officers think that all people are the same and they can't get out of that tunnel vision way of thinking. It can happen, especially when policemen work in low income areas. It happened to Officer Shawn. He treated citizens like they were beneath him and he always felt that it was the police against the people.

I never adhered to this theory. I was raised and educated and now live in Washington, DC. I loved my city and the different type of people that lived there. I knew them and knew many good people lived in the city. I was trained to treat people the same, no matter where they resided.

I have learned that the majority of the people who reside in low income areas are good people and they support and believe in their police department. I also learned that people in these areas demand that policemen treat them better and they watch everything that you do. Officer Shawn did exactly the contrary; he treated people like they were beneath him.

I was a young officer and didn't have much authority when addressing issues of this magnitude. During those times as a policeman, your time in grade was important and everyone treated you according to your time on the job. No one would listen to me because of my time on the job. Officer Shawn had time on the job and that was the way it was.

Officer Shawn did teach me one important thing. If you continued to do bad things and walk that fine line of good and evil, it will catch up to you in time.

I also learned that when policemen are allowed by their superiors or fellow officers to break the rules and constantly get away with bad decisions, it is the officer that will suffer the immediate punishment of society and the police department will suffer the mistrust of the community. Once you lose the trust of the community, it takes a long time to get it back.

Officer Shawn had a girlfriend name Ronnie that lived in an apartment in Southeast, Washington, DC. Officer Shawn was very jealous of Ronnie and sometimes even cruel to her because of his fear that she might leave him. It was rumored by other police officers that Ronnie dated other policemen, even police women. I never confirmed that fact, because I didn't socialize in those circles. I just listened to the other police officer's talk.

It was a very warm Monday and my section was about to check off. Officer Shawn walk out the roll call room in a hurry, telling the other officers that he wouldn't be joining them at the drinking hole tonight. This is where all the police officers went to drink liquor, every night. After two months of doing this, I told myself that this type of life wasn't for me.

My section consisted of 20 police officers and most of them had bad lives and were unhappy. I wanted more from life than just drinking every night and trying to get laid. I didn't go with the other officers that night. I went home and started studying for the police sergeant's exam. I wanted to be a sergeant.

I reported to work the next day and everyone in the police district was talking about Officer Shawn. It appears that after leaving work the day before, Officer Shawn went over to Ronnie's apartment. She had called him and reported that her next-door neighbor, Michael Williams, had pushed her as they were entering their front door of their apartment building that morning. We later learned that it was an accident; Michael just didn't apologize to Ronnie. She must have interrupted the incident as an assault on her. Apparently, after being advised of the incident by Ronnie, Officer Shawn went to Michael's apartment, entered the same, and beat him almost to death with his hands. He left Michael inside the apartment, which was only two doors from Ronnie on the same floor,

During the attack, witnesses observing the attack called the police. On their arrival, the police found Michael bleeding inside his apartment.

The witnesses identified Officer Shawn as the attacker and identified his location. Further investigation resulted in Officer Shawn's arrest.

After learning the facts, I wasn't surprised. I knew Officer Shawn and I suspected that one day he would explode. He was a walking time bomb and Ronnie lighted the fuse. It didn't take much. I just didn't understand why Officer Shawn could think that he could beat someone so savagely and get away with the crime. Maybe he thought that by being a police officer, nothing would happen to him. He was mistaken.

During the trial, Officer Shawn claimed that Michael had attack him and he was defending himself. There were too many holes in his story and he was charged with several crimes. He was found guilty and served twenty years in jail.

Michael survived the attack but lost his left eye.

Ronnie relocated and I never saw her again.

Officer Mark Shawn 1978

I didn't like or respect Officer Shawn and I learned what not to be as a police officer and that was an Officer Shawn.

My First Police Shooting 1978

Chapter 26

I had just left roll call and it was a beautiful Thursday evening. I was standing behind the police district waiting for my relief to bring the police cruiser in. I was assigned to Scout Car 182. Immediately after entering my scout car, I received a radio assignment for an injured person.

The address was 800 Barnaby Road S.E. and I knew the address well. It was a very quiet apartment and mostly senior citizens lived in the building. I first thought that someone fell down the steps. I had no idea what I was about to face!

Scout Car 183 with Officer John Lacey, was assigned to back me up. I acknowledge the dispatcher and drove right to the address, I felt that it would be a milk run, easy.

On my arrival, I observed several people running out the building. As I exited my vehicle I saw a man, later identified as Mr. Frank Smith, lying down in the hallway bleeding from the head. It appeared that he had been struck by some object.

Mr. Smith said, "That crazy fucker hit me with a baseball bat. He is inside that apartment" He was pointing to apartment #101. The door was open.

I radioed the dispatcher and advised him of the situation and I requested an ambulance.

As I entered the apartment, Officer Lacey walked in behind me and said, "Kittrell, I am behind you."

I said, "About time." I was kidding. I should have waited for Lacey before responding to the scene. That was the end of my milk run.

We heard noise in the only bedroom and walk very cautiously down the small hallway towards the room. At the time the hallway appeared to be very long. We reached the door and we observed a very large man, later identified as a Mr. Frank Wildered, sitting on the edge of the bed, with no clothes on. I said, *oh my God, this isn't going to turn out well.*

Officer Lacey enters the bedroom and walks to my right. I move to the left as to corner Mr. Wildered. Before we could say anything, Mr. Wildered stood up and said, "Do you know who I am? Do you know who I am? I am the son of God!" He then ran out the bedroom and opened the closet in the hallway and removed a baseball bat. There was still blood on it.

Mr. Wildered started swinging the bat and said, "I am going to kill you!" He ran towards us, swinging the bat. By this time, I had removed my revolver and pointed the same at Mr.

My First Police Shooting 1978

Wildered. I ordered him to drop the bat, several times. Realizing that we were about to be struck by the bat and knowing the seriousness of an assault by a bat, I fired my revolver twice, striking Mr. Wildered twice in the chest.

Mr. Wildered fell to the floor looking at me, saying, "You fucker! You shot me!"

I didn't say anything. Lacey called for an ambulance and requested assistance. We attempted to stop the bleeding, but in a very short period an ambulance crew had arrived and took over. I wasn't so surprise at how fast they arrives, because we were only a few blocks away from the hospital in S.E Washington, DC.

Even though Mr. Wildered attempted to seriously hurt my partner and me, I didn't want him to die. He was a human being and somebody's son, maybe even a father.

I always knew that as a police officer on any given day, you might be put in a situation that would call upon you to take someone's life. This was my day. Mr. Wildered wasn't looking good. I have seen many gunshot victims and the ones that didn't make it always looked the same. They had a look of someone looking into the unknown knowing they were in that place and they didn't want to be there. I said a prayer for him as they put him in the ambulance. Twenty minutes later, I was informed that Mr. Wildered had died.

In Washington, DC, whenever a police officer is involved in a police shooting and someone dies, the Homicide

Branch handles the investigation; this was my first time ever being exposed to such a dramatic investigation. I always had respect for the Homicide Detectives. They were good at their job and it made me want to be a Homicide Detective.

I remember when I applied for a position in the branch a few years earlier. To be a detective, you must take a test and I did very well. When the opening was announced I immediately applied for the position and had an interview. On that day, I learned a great deal how the Metropolitan Police Department operates.

I walked into the interview room and I was met by the captain who ran the branch. He had 29 years on the job. There were also two lieutenants on the panel. They each had 24 years of experience as policemen. I was very impress with the panel. As I told the panel about myself and the reason for wanting the job, I really felt good they might just pick me. Once I concluded my presentation, the captain's words at first hurt, but later they motivated me.

The captain said, "Officer Kittrell, I admire your test score and it appears that you know your police books and you have a clean record. But, it takes more than book knowledge to become a Homicide Detective. Look around at my officers. All those guys in that room have 20 years of experience, working as detectives in the field before coming to the Homicide Branch. That is the reason for us being number one in the country, experience.

My First Police Shooting 1978

I am not telling you that you don't have the experience to become a good detective. You just need more time on the job before coming in this office. I applaud you for attempting to become a Homicide Detective.

I thanked the captain for being honest and for seeing me. I was hurt at first, but he planted a fire in me that lasted throughout my police career. He was upright and suggested that I pursue a career as a supervisor, in that my scores were so high. The captain's words also reinforced my thoughts about the Homicide Branch; they were the best in the country.

As I was giving my statement to the Homicide Detectives, I really felt they were about business and wanted the truth. They went over my story with a fine tooth comb and I felt good about it.

When I left their office, the sergeant in the branch grabbed my hands and said, "Officer Kittrell, you did your duty and I am glad that you are going home to your family tonight. Everything will be okay."

I felt very strange when I gave my revolver to the police technicians for processing as evidence. This is the normal procedure in such cases. I was then directed to go to Communications Division to get a new revolver. The next day, I went to the Property Division and was issued a new revolver and turn the old revolver back in, that was the process.

The senior officers always told the young officers, that one of the strangest feelings for a police officer is to be relieved of his revolver and police identification. It' makes you feel that you are no longer a police officer. It did to me. I have even known police officers to cry.

I went home, kissed my family, and took a very long shower to think about what just happen. I really didn't want to kill anyone, but I wasn't about to die in the line of duty, unless that was the only option open for me to do my job. I wanted to see my children grow up and I wanted to have grandchildren. I wanted to retire and have a long and proactive life with my family.

Four months later, I was sitting inside a Grand Jury Hearing and my case was presented to them. Whenever a police officer kills someone, the case is submitted to the Grand Jury for their investigation and finding. The Homicide Detective presented the case to the jury and responded to their questions. There were three questions. The hearing lasted approximately 20 minutes, but it felt like a lifetime because sometimes juries are very tricky and do things that you never thought about.

My lieutenant called me at home the next day and said the jury found my shooting justified and I was scheduled to return to work in two weeks. I thanked the lieutenant and felt good that the system worked. On my return to work, I was greeted by my fellow officers and it made me feel like I was part of a family. I was glad I could return to my family.

Out on my own
1978
Chapter 27

"We may part, but never will I ever be shocked again"
LT Marco F. Kittrell, MPDC, (ret)

It was Christmas eve, snowing, and one of the quietest evenings that I ever worked. People were on the way home, gifts in hand, laughing, and some singing. Children were so excited. They were chasing each other and throwing snow balls. I said, *what could go wrong on a night like this?* I was in for a surprise.

At 8:30 p.m., my partner and I, Officer Curtis Columbus, received an assignment for "assist the citizen with clothes." We referred to this as a clothes run. The address was 2734 Livingston Terrace #102, Southeast. I knew this address. It was a quiet street and we normally didn't receive radio runs to that location.

When we arrived at the apartment the scenery looked like a post card for Christmas. There were no imprints in the snow. You could see people through their windows preparing for Christmas; placing gifts under the Christmas tree, cooking in the kitchen. There were Christmas lights all over the apartment building. I said, *what could be wrong here?*

We knocked on the door and could here Christmas music coming from the apartment. A young man, who was later identified as Mr. George Starke, opened the door.

Mr. Starks was wearing a black robe, smoking a cigar, and holding a glass of scotch in his hand. Mr. Starks asked, "Officer, how can I help you. No one here called the police"

Mr. Starks turns towards a young lady, who later was identified as Ms. Joan White, sitting on the couch and asked if she had called the police.

Ms. White came to the door and said, "Yes, officer. Please come in. I called the police."

Mr. Starks asked, did anybody threaten you?

Ms. White replied, "No."

"Then, what is the problem? Why do you have these officers at our apartment on Christmas Eve?" asked Mr. Starks.

Ms. White's next comments not only surprise me but established the way that I think now, concerning such incidents.

Ms. White looked at Mr. Starks and told him that her girlfriend told Ms. White that Mr. Starks had been looking for an apartment to live in by himself. She further stated that if he wanted to leave, he could leave right now.

Mr. Starks told Ms. White that they were staying together until he had located a place to live and this was temporary.

Ms. Whites told my partner and me that, she rented the apartment and presented a lease which indicated the same. She told us that they have been living together for only two months, which isn't considered common law marriage under the District of Columbia. She said she wanted Mr. Starks to leave now. He was to take off her robe that she had purchased, stop smoking her cigar, don't drink another drop of her scotch, and take only the things that he brought into the apartment, which wasn't that much.

As a final insult, Ms. White said that she wanted back the underwear that Mr. Starks was wearing; she paid for them and they weren't a gift.

Mr. Starks looked at the woman as if he is in shock, and says, "Baby, what happened? Where did all this come from?"

"You know where it came from," she responded. "Officers, escort this gentleman off the property, now." She took the glass out of his hand and threw the liquor in the sink.

I don't want Mr. Starks to go off and make the incident any worse that it is. I advise Mr. Stark that Ms. White was in her legal rights and he was required to leave.

Mr. Starks looked like he was about to cry. "Five minutes ago, I was eating steak and chocolate cake and drinking 12-year-old scotch. That bitch gave me a good bath, greased my hair, and fucked me like a French whore. I was smoking a $25.00 cigar and wearing a $100 robe and now I am on the street like a beggar." The he started crying.

Mr. Starks went into the bathroom, took off the underwear, left the clothes on the floor and grabbed what cloths he had; they all fit into one trash bag. We escorted Mr. Starks outside. Ms. White slammed the door behind us, looked through the window, and closed the blind. I said, *what a coldhearted woman.*

It was like a movie. It started snowing much heavier as we walked towards the police cruiser. Mr. Starks stated, "I have nowhere to go."

I suggested the men's shelter. It was his only option that night, in that Mr. Starks had no money, no friends, and no relatives in the area.

As we were driving towards the men's shelter, located in down town Washington, DC, Mr. Starks told us the whole story. He met Ms. White four months ago. He had just relocated to Washington, DC to work in the federal government and she offered him a place to live until he got himself together. I guess she had other plans and she forgot to tell Mr. Starks.

We finally reach the men's shelter, it looks like hell.

Several men were sitting out front as if they have just been released from jail. Mr. Starks look through the window of the police vehicle as if to say, *how did I end up here?*

He exited the vehicle. With his head hanging down and carrying the trash bag with all his clothes, he walks up the steps and starts crying as he reaches the door.

He stopped. One of the residents opened the door for him and said, "Mother-fucker, don't come in here with all that sad shit on Christmas Eve. You will fuck it up for everyone. If you don't like it, get the fuck out. Some bitch must have thrown you out tonight. You can always tell. You mother-fuckers are always crying."

Mr. Stark's stopped crying and walked into the shelter and that was the last time that I saw him.

This one incident dictated my thinking to the present day; *God bless the child that has his own.*

My Sister

1978

Chapter 28

"May my sister forgive me for my sins for my sin will not forgive me"
LT Marco F. Kittrell, MPDC, (ret)

It was 11:30 a.m., and I received a radio assignment for a stabbing at 934 Wade Road, Southeast. On my arrival, I see that the ambulance had already arrived and other police units.

Once in the house, I see two police officers attempting to subdue a young girl, later identified as Janice, who appeared to be approximately 16 years old or younger. There are also several people attempting to stop the police officers from arresting her. I immediately jump into the uproar and pull the people off the police officers.

During this time, the ambulance crew is working on a young girl, later identified as Toni, who is lying on the floor. She has a large knife imbedded in her chest. Several of the people in the house are yelling at Janice asking, "Why you stabbed your sister?"

The house is very small and we are attempting not to step on Toni as the firemen are working on her and attempting to stabilize her. I could see that Toni is unconscious and maybe dying. Another two police officers enter the house and with their assistance we were then able to subdue everyone in the home.

Two police officers place handcuffs on Janice, take her outside, and placed her in the police cruiser. Prior to exiting the house Janice looks at Toni and said, "Bitch I hope you die! Sister or not, I don't give a shit, bitch!"

Two more firemen arrive and began assisting the other firemen in treating Toni. Once the firemen stabilized Toni, they transport her to the hospital. A short time later, Toni succumbed to her wounds and died.

Once everyone inside the house has been subdued, the parents of Janice and Toni started crying and saying where they have gone wrong with their children.

During the investigation, we learned that the sisters were arguing over a dress that Toni had borrowed from Janice. Toni refuse to take the dress off and an argument ensued where Janice stabbed Toni with a butcher knife.

Janice was charged as an adult with Murder II. In Washington, DC, if a child between the ages of 16 and 17 commits certain crimes they can be charged as adults. Janice pled guilty at trial and was sentence to twenty years. Janice was released from prison in 1990, married, and had two children. Janice's parents lived with Janice and her family.

The Unusual Burglary Suspects
1979
Chapter 29

I was working the midnight shift and working as a 10-99 unit, which is a one-man unit. It was Saturday night and we were short staffed, like most Saturday nights on midnights.

At approximately 2:30 a.m., I received an assignment for a burglary that just occurred. On my arrival, I was met by a Mr. and Mrs. Charles Smith. Once I entered the house, I immediately noticed that the house was very clean and organized. I ask Mr. Smith what happen. He informed me that his home had been burglarized and at the time of the entry he and his wife were at home. There were three men and they had tied the Smiths to a chair as they burglarized their home.

As they were talking to me, I knew something was wrong. I had learned that sometimes, when a house is burglarized and a female is at home at the time of the entry, the women could have been raped. The Smiths were giving me this feeling that his wife had been assaulted. They were both looking down to the floor as they spoke with me and didn't answer my entire question fully. It acted if they were either hiding something or as if they were ashamed of what happen.

Sometimes, victims of a crime feel wounded and go into what I call a shock process. This is when a person is in a daze and can't believe what has happened.

I took Mr. Smith to the side, in that I didn't want to embarrass him in front of his wife, and asked if his wife was assaulted by the suspects. Mr. Smith grabbed my arm, looked at me in my eyes and said, "No, officer, they assaulted me and sodomize me."

This was the first time that I was confronted with such a situation. It took a couple of seconds to compose myself and I ask Mr. Smith to tell me what happen, if he could.

He stated that as he and his wife were sleeping, the suspects entering through the basement window and walked up to their bedroom and tied them up with duct tape.

It was then that the suspects untied Mr. Smith, took him to the next bedroom, and all three suspects sodomize him. After the assault, they left Mr. Smith tied up in the same bedroom.

During the burglary, the suspects stole several items from the home and made good their escape byway of the rear door.

As I was talking to Mr. Smith, I noticed that it was very difficult for him. He talked as a man who was so ashamed. I attempted to comfort him, but he wasn't receiving my comments.

I call for the assistance of a detective and ambulance. Further investigation revealed that the suspects had committed several other burglaries in the Washington, DC, area and the men weren't reporting the incidents. The detectives reached out to other detectives in the area and inquired if they had had similar incidents. The detectives back tracked on some of their old cases and the information was revealed. Men weren't reporting the cases.

Three months later, due to good detective work, evidence was located by the detectives and the three suspects were identified.

The suspects never gave a reason for the unusual behavior. The suspects were charged with nine cases of burglaries and assault.

I learned early in as a police officer that you must really work hard at your trade, if you are to be successful. Never think that the obvious is factual, because no matter what you are confronted with it might only be a mirage.

People who are middle class citizens always have a hard time when they are the victim of certain crimes. In this case, all the men felt ashamed that they were victims of such a hennas crime.

This is not so uncommon among women when they are victims of assaults.

Trying to Make a Living

1979

Chapter 30

> "I am a troubled man with a troubled past, will my past be my future?"
> LT Marco F. Kittrell, MPDC, (ret)

It was Friday morning at 9:30 am and three men were working in a house that they had purchased. The house needed repairs and they were planning to refurbish the same and sell for a profit. The three men had formed a company and named it after themselves. MTA Construction Company, which stood for Michael, Thomas, and Antony. This was their third project together and they had been very successful. They were even planning to expand the company.

All three men were under thirty and they all grew up together as friends. They attended the same schools and church and their parents knew each other. They even married three women that were all in the same family. They and their families were very close, even taking vacations together.

On this day, like any other day, things were going well. They had just completed a major portion of the project and were having lunch on the first floor of the house.

As they are eating, three young men walk into the house and produced hand guns. The suspects stated that this was a hold-up and directed Michael, Thomas, and Anthony to walk down to the basement. Anthony tells the robbery suspects that he and his friends are just trying to make a living, like everybody else. This isn't necessary and they don't have any money. Anthony is unaware of the type of people that he is dealing with; career criminals with violent backgrounds.

The three suspects were later identified as Mike, Warren, and Terry. In response to Anthony's remarks, Warren strikes Anthony with a pistol to his face causing several lacerations. This was only the beginning. Michael and Thomas attempted to assist their friend, but the other suspects told them that if they took another step they would both be shot dead. It was at that time the three friends knew they were dealing with dangerous people. Anthony tells his friends that he was okay and please don't do anything that would endanger anyone.

Michael, Thomas, and Anthony start walking towards the door that led to the basement. As Michael opens the door, he looks at his friend, as if to say, *if we go down those stairs, we will not come back up.*

By being friends for so many years, they could read each other's body language. Unfortunately, professional criminals are also good at reading body language. That is a key to their survival on the streets. Not understanding a person's movements is a quick and true way to be killed or jailed. These suspects were experience criminals and knew what to do when cornered. They weren't going to be in a fix, in a spot as not being able to maneuver.

Warren tells the three friends, "I hope you are not thinking about not following our directions. That is a one-way ticket to hell. All we want is your money. Don't be no fools or we will kill you."

Thomas later told us, the police, that when he looked in their eyes it was like looking at tigers about to jump on a lamb. Their eyes were cold and looked right through them. We were determined to see our families that night and once Warren made those statements, we knew what we had to do; survive.

Michael was the first person to take the initiative. He grabbed one of the suspects, but is shot once in head and falls to the floor, immediately, taking the suspect with him as he is holding onto him.

Thomas, who was the bigger man of the three friends, pushed the other two suspects to the floor. Unfortunately, Thomas was also shot in the stomach, causing him to fall to the ground.

Anthony picks up a hammer and started beating the three suspects repeatedly, yelling and calling the suspects animals and other vulgar names. During the altercation, Thomas was also shot twice in the chest, but he still subdued the suspects and prevented them from shooting his friends any further.

A witness heard the gun fire and called the police. On our arrival, I observed what could only be related to as the shootout at the OK Corral. I ran into the house. Bodies were lying all over the floor and everyone was bleeding profusely. Michael and Thomas were not moving. We first thought they were dead.

The ambulance crews arrived and started working on the injured as we, the police, attempted to unravel what happen. Thomas was the only person able to give us an account of the incident. As the ambulance crew was attending to Thomas's injury, he told us the story, while yelling in pain, but we finally gathered the facts.

The three suspects were seriously injured. Mike was later classified as brain dead, Warren went into a coma, and Terry lost his left eye.

A hammer is a very dangerous weapon and it doesn't take very much to cause injury when striking someone with it. Thomas was attempting to defend his friends and himself. Thomas later said that all he could see was his family and he wanted to live for them.

The three suspects were all charged with attempted murder and other charges; they were given 25 years to life as a sentence. Mike and Warren died the following year, succumbing to their injuries.

Michael, Thomas, and Anthony all recovered from their wounds and continued their business. The incident changed their lives, but not their belief and aspirations.

The House Fire
1979
Chapter 31

It was a rainy and cold night and I was about to get off duty. It was 10:30 p.m. and I wanted to go home and get in the bed. It had been a hard and long day, plus I had been in court for 8 hours. I couldn't wait to get into my bed.

As I am approaching the police district, I get the call. The dispatcher asks if any units are in service and able to take a radio assignment. I immediately advise the dispatcher that I could handle the assignment. I had thirty more minutes before I was relieved from duty; what the hell.

The dispatcher informed me that the fire department was responding to 3645-Wheeler Road SE for the house on fire. I volunteered for the assignment and started driving towards the location.

As I approached the location, I could see a large amount of smoke coming from the house. The fire department was already on the scene and started fighting the fire. As I exited my vehicle, I couldn't believe the amount of smoke and fire. The entire house was engulfed in fire.

I said to myself; *with all this rain, the fire is just out of control and it look like one big barn fire.* I couldn't believe the amount of people that were standing in the rain, just watching the fire.

I knew people like watching house fires, but I could never figure that out. Cold, rain, smoke, and the wind blowing like a hurricane. It was a bad scene.

I walked up to the fire department captain and asked how long it would take to get the fire under control. The captain tells me that it will take a while, a long while. The police could help by just keeping the people back and out of the way. I just smiled and said, "Okay."

It took the fire department approximately two hours to get the fire under control. I must admit, I was somewhat taking back by the fire and the way the fire department handle the situation. I always respected the fire department. They knew what they were doing and very good at their job. They always went by the numbers when dealing with fire and other emergencies.

Once the fire was under control, the fire department captain approached me and told me to follow him. He said, "Officer, you will not believe this shit."

He doesn't tell me anything but he is walking very fast and tells his firemen to keep everybody back. The captain gave me a fire helmet and gas mask to wear and told me to watch my steps. I couldn't believe I was able to walk inside the house.

We snaked our way through the house and the captain points to the kitchen. I walked in and I saw a middle aged man lying on the floor, dead. The captain tells me that the man is dead. His people have already attempted to revive him, but he is gone. He says, "You now have a homicide on your hands, officer," and walks away.

I immediately advise the dispatcher and request for a homicide unit to respond. On their arrival and after investigating, it was learned that the deceased was a Mr. John Adams, who resided at the residence. Mr. Adams succumbed to a knife wound to the back of his neck.

Further investigation lead to suspecting his wife, who wasn't on the scene. The detectives followed their leads and they led to Ms. Adams' sister's address, which was only four blocks away.

We drove to the address and knocked on the door. Ms. Adams' sister answered the door and asked what we wanted. The detectives asked if Ms. Adams was in the house and said they wanted to speak with her. She gave her approval. We entered the home and saw Ms. Adams seated on the couch watching television.

Before the detectives could say anything, Ms. Adams started crying and asked how her husband was doing. The detectives didn't say anything. They wanted Mrs. Adams to talk as much as she wanted before they said anything to her. They just gazed at Ms. Adams. She continued to cry. A minute goes by.

Ms. Adams stood up, looked at the detective and said, "That mother-fucker wasn't shit and I am glad that he is dead. I wish him a happy life in hell."

Ms. Adams further stated that her husband was a drunk and beat on her and she was tired of all the crap. Today her husband came home, pushed her down, and kicked her. As he walked away, she grabbed a knife and stabbed him in the neck. She panicked and started the fire to hide the murder.

We arrested Ms. Adams. She was charged with murder and she pled guilty during the trial. She was sentenced to 15 years, but she only served 3 years. The Adams' had three children and they were raised by their grandparents, the mother's parents.

I just wanted to go home and get some sleep that day. I didn't make it home until the next day.

I loved my job.

My Second Police Shooting 1979

Chapter 32

    I was working with Officer Tyron Times. He was a very funny guy and loved the idea about being a police officer. His father and grandfather were both retired police officers from Chicago and he was always trying to live up to their expectations. Sometimes, I thought he took to many risks.

    Officer Times was very good at recognizing stolen vehicles. There was no one better at it than him. He could look at a car and say, "That's a stolen car," and every time we checked, the car was stolen. I thought he had some type of gift. Officer Times would recover three cars a week and that was on a bad week.

    He and I were in so many car chases, I wouldn't eat any food until at the end of the shift. I got tired of throwing my food away in the police car. I would start eating my food and at that time Officer Times would spot a stolen vehicle and the chase was on.

It was approximately 7:30 p.m. and Officer Times and I were transporting a prisoner to the DC jail. During the entire day, Officer Times had me laughing all day, making jokes about everything and everybody.

I told him he should write a book about some of the stories. He said he would, but he didn't think his father and grandfather would approve. Officer Times wanted his family to respect his accomplishments as they did his father and grandfather. I told him that in my family we were raised to be your own man and live your own dreams and still respect your family.

We had transported numerous prisoners to jail on many occasions, but on this day, Officer Times kept making wrong turns and we were going in circles. We found ourselves traveling northbound on 17Th Street, approaching East Capitol Street; I started laughing and said, "Man, can you please get us to the jail before next year."

It was at that moment, we drove by an apartment building. Officer Times said, "Kittrell, man with a gun." and he stoped the vehicle and started exiting it. I looked in his direction and saw a man, later identified as a Mr. James Woodson, with a German luger, pointing the weapon at another man's head.

I could hear Mr. Woodson saying, "If you don't give me my damn money, I will blow your head off."

Officer Times and I reached the front of the building at the same time. There were three steps, for some unknown reason, and I always thank God for my next action. We stopped at the first step at the same time. We had drawn our service revolvers and pointed the same at Mr. Woodson. My gun is pointing right at Mr. Woodson, my finger is on the trigger, and according to my training I said, "Police!" That was all I could say. Mr. Woodson turned around and fired three shots at Officer Times and me.

If we would have been on the second step the shots would have struck us, but by being on the first step, I felt those rounds go over my head and next to both ears. I even believed I saw the rounds come at me. After a couple seconds, my brain finally told my hand that this man was trying to kill us and I fired two shots at Mr. Woodson. I believe Officer Times fired twice also. Two rounds struck Mr. Woodson in the face, causing him to fall.

This was the only the beginning of our problems. After shooting Mr. Woodson, several citizens in the neighbor gathered very quickly. They all started shouting, "Those pigs shot Little James!"

Some of the people picked up rocks and started throwing the rocks at us. I grabbed the German Luger that Mr. Woodson had held and we ran into the apartment building, positioned ourselves in the hallway. We couldn't lose the evidence. Under normal conditions, we wouldn't have moved the evidence, but the crowd would have probably stolen the item. That was the main evidence that we had to show that we were fired upon.

Officer Times has already advised the dispatcher and requested back-up. We could hear the sirens from the police cars, but it appeared that they were miles away. The mob started throwing rocks inside the hallway where we had positioned ourselves. Officer Times then said, "Marco, we left the prisoner in the police car."

"No we didn't. He is standing behind you," I said. "How in the hell did he get here?"

I had grabbed the prisoner once safe guarding the weapon. Officer Times was so concern with the mob and things happen so fast, he didn't see what I had done.

The prisoner asks, "What are we going to do?"

Officer Times replied, "If we die, you are going to die too."

The prisoner looks at Officer Times and said, "Not me. You are the damn police and I am a damn prisoner. Remove these damn handcuffs and I will help you guys."

We both said, "Hell no!"

In that God was looking over us, I could see police red lights as they appeared in the apartment building.

Officer Times said, "It's about fucking time."

The officers started moving the crowd back and one officer, Sergeant Ronald Jenkins, yelled into the apartment building, "Kittrell! Times! Police! Coming in!"

My Second Police Shooting 1980

Sergeant Jenkins walked into the hallway with his hands in his pockets smoking a cigarette, saying, after removing the cigarette, "I was eating my dinner and talking to my wife about our new granddaughter, and then I heard this shit, over the radio. Are you guys okay?"

We both acknowledge the sergeant by saying, "Yes sir!"

"Okay let's get cleaned up. You know the drill. This shit!"

The technician walks behind the sergeant and we begin telling our story. We turn the German Luger over to the technicians. Mr. Woodson is pronounced dead on the scene and the homicide detectives arrived and began their work of investigating the incident.

In that this was my second shooting, I knew what to expect. Once Officer Times and I were released by the Homicide Branch we went to my house and had several drinks. During the conversation, we both said how lucky we were to be alive. If we would have been on the second step, one or both of us could be dead.

It just wasn't our time. That was the first conversation that Officer Times and I had without making jokes or laughing at each other. We had our last drink and I told the officer I would see him next week

He asked, since this was my second shooting, what should he expect. I explain the process and he appeared to be surprised that he would be off duty for a few months. He thought that was too long and we would be considered guilty by the other police. I further explain that it was the process and don't worry about it. We were innocent and don't worry about other people. It wasn't important. That kind of thinking was harmful to ones dignity. As we continued talking, Officer Times started talking about his wife. He said how much he didn't like her. She was a drunk, very lazy, didn't clean the house, wasn't a good mother, gambled all his money away, and refused to have sex with him. Now this caught me completely off guard.

Then it hit me, Officer Times never talked about his immediately family. His father and grandfather were the only ones he mentioned of his family, never wife or children. After hearing how much he disliked his wife, I clearly understood why. I asked, "If you are so unhappy, why don't you get a divorce?"

He said, "Kittrell, I wish it was that easy, but it just isn't, man."

I didn't go any further on that topic. It wasn't my place to tell a man to divorce his wife and leave his family. I just didn't like it when people grumble about something and don't do anything about the problem. That was what I was hearing.

We were both off from work for approximately two months and we talked weekly on the phone. I always felt like he wanted to tell me something, but he would never complete the story.

My Second Police Shooting 1980

On our first week back at work, Officer Times and I were eating breakfast and he just looked at me and said, "Man, I'm going to get a divorce from my wife. That's it. I'm going to do it."

I said, "I wish you and your family luck. Just think things through. Divorce isn't easy and they are hard on the family, especially children."

Officer Times said, "I don't care. I am not happy. I hate my wife and I am going to be happy.

That was the end of the conversation. Within 12 months he divorced his wife and started dated another policewoman. They married and are still together today.

After this shooting, I approached every incident more cautiously and always attempted to keep my guard up. I felt God saved me and wanted me to do something. This was just too close for comfort and I had seen too many policemen killed or seriously hurt. I wanted to "be there" for my family.

This event made me more appreciative of life, especially family, my children. I was a young man and I didn't want my children going through life without their father. They needed a man, their father, in their life and they had a long way to go. I made it my mission to be there for them. I wanted to see them married, see them have children, and enjoy life like my parents did, who observed their children growing up.

I didn't want to change the way I did my job. I believed I was doing a good job and I had a large amount of experience to offer, even thou I was still very young.

I just needed to make sure that I did everything my teachers taught me and my experience was used in a way to better myself and others.

I thank God for allowing me to be here today and giving me the foresight to make the correct decisions when confronted with such difficult choices. There will be many more before it was all over.

The Dentist Office
1980
Chapter 33

I had a dentist appointment at 9 am and the dentist office was in Southwest Washington. I had missed two prior appointments and I wasn't going to miss this one. I was scheduled to report to work at 3p.m. and I felt my dentist appointment wouldn't be more than two hours, giving me plenty of time to report to work.

I walked into the dentist office and the nurse immediately said, "Mr. Kittrell, the doctor is waiting for you."

This was good timing and I might leave earlier. I left my coat in the waiting room with my police identification folder and badge in my coat. This was a mistake that I would soon learn. I normally wouldn't make such a mistake, but I wasn't thinking and I was rushing. As a policeman, you should never rush and always think about what you are doing, always. I should have known better, but I did keep my service revolver with me.

The doctor told me to get in the chair and asked, "How are things going in the police department?"

I said, "Fine. I am studying for the sergeant's exam."

The dentist gave me some encouraging words towards my goal and was about to give me a shot to prepare for the tooth removal.

He said, "Officer Kittrell, let me get my nurse to assist with the removal."

I said, "Ok doctor, Take your time."

The dentist left the office and as I was lying there for a few seconds, I heard the dentist say, "Just do what he says."

I wasn't sure and before I could turn my head a young man was pointing a gun in my face, telling me, "Don't move or I will shoot you."

I immediately said to myself, *I don't believe after five years on the police force I allow myself to be caught off-guard and some punk is pointing a gun in my face. I am a police officer and I am screwed today.*

He pulled me out of the chair and threw me down on the floor. My gun is inside my waist band beneath my sweater. The suspect doesn't see the weapon. In my mind I am thinking, *I am going to shoot this punk, at the first opportunity*. Then a second suspect enters the room

Suspect 2, "Don't spend a lot of time with this man and let's get the drugs."

Suspect 1 ties my hand behind my back, with my face lying down to the ground.

The Dentist Office 1980

Suspect 2 brings the dentist and the nurse into the room. Their hands have been tied behind their backs and they also are thrown to the floor next to me, their faces lying on the floor.

I tell them, "Just remain calm." and ask, "Are there any more suspects in the house."

They shake their heads, "No."

The two suspects ransack the dentist's office looking for money and medication. They know what kind of medication they are looking for in that they have already questioned the dentist and are aware of the contents and its location.

As I am lying on the floor, helpless and fearing that the suspect would recognize me as a policeman, I attempt to undo my hands, without any success. The dentist attempts to sway me not to take any action that would enrage the suspects. I ask him to keep watch and warn me when the suspects return. He continues to tell me not to take any actions that would incite the situation. In my mind, I know what criminals can do and having seen their brutality. I wasn't going to allow myself to become another victim.

I had seen to many people killed, cut, burned, and seriously injured by thugs, to do nothing. The dentist hadn't, I assumed, but you never know a person's experiences until you talk to them. I had learned that much in my short police career. The way the dentist was acting gave me some insight into the man. He wanted to play it safe and hope nothing happened. I knew better. Criminals live on others weakness and they can smell fear and make their living on such thinking.

By talking to the dentist, I lost vital time. I put so much time in talking to the dentist that I stopped what I was doing and let the suspects make their way back into our room. They looked at me and I realized they knew I was a policeman.

Suspect 1 said, "We know that you are a cop and we want your weapon."

The two suspects gave me a look of disgust and as if to say, "The last thing you will see is us, your executioners."

I said a very quick prayer to myself and said, *I made a big mistake, talking too long to the dentist, and it was going to cost me my life.*

I couldn't believe I could make such a tragic mistake. I thought about my children and didn't realize how great they were, until you almost loose them.

Suspect 1 goes to my waist band and removes my weapon. Then he takes his weapon and points the same to my head and pulls the trigger. No discharge. The gun malfunctioned. Suspect 2 said, "Let's go. We have been here to long. Let that mother fucker go."

Suspect 1 then kicked me in my stomach. It wasn't much of a kick, but I didn't say anything. I just made a very loud noise acknowledging the assault. The two suspects then ran out the office with my service weapon, police credentials, and brand-new coat.

The Dentist Office 1980

The nurse was the first person that stood up. Apparently, the suspects didn't tie her hands very securely and she was able to break free. She then untied the dentist and I was finally set free. I immediately thanked God and then look at the dentist with some disgust, thinking *he almost got me killed*. But, I soon came to my senses and said *it wasn't anyone's fault*. It just happens and I should be thankful that the suspect gun malfunctioned and I wasn't killed.

The dentist looked at me and as he attempted to say something. I just grabbed him and said, "Let's check on your family and make sure they are ok."

The dentist office was in the basement of his townhouse. In this part of town, which was a very high income area, this was normal for many professionals such as doctors, lawyers, architects, and other professionals.

The suspects never made their way upstairs and the dentist's family was never endangered. His wife and two little children ran down stairs and grabbed him saying, "Daddy, are you ok? We were scared. The bad men said they were going to kill us if we came down the stairs."

During the original confusion, the dentist's wife came down the stairs and the suspect made her lay on the steps, without hurting her. She had observed the entire ordeal. As she lay on the steps, she held her two children in her arms, pleading with the suspects not to hurt her family.

I heard this as the dentist was attempting to stop me from breaking lose and attack the suspects. I knew what could have happened and it didn't. We were lucky and God gave us another chance.

When I saw the dentist and his family holding each other, I just figured the dentist was attempting to safeguard his family and that was the most important thing to him at the time. His family came first and he wanted to protect them the best way he knew.

I was a policeman and I wanted to apprehend the suspects or even kill them. We had two different agendas. My training directed that I act in a certain way when confronted with certain situations and that was exactly what I was going to do.

The two suspects were apprehended two days later as they attempted to rob a grocery store by gun point in Southeast, Washington.

They even used my stolen weapon to commit the robbery. There was a small shootout and the suspects lost. Both men were shot during the commission of the robbery, but neither wound was serious.

During the investigation, it was learned that the suspects had committed approximately forty armed robberies in the Washington Metropolitan area within a five-month period. I later learned that the suspects had been targeting dentist offices.

The Dentist Office 1980

In my instance, if I had been aware of that information, I might have been more prepared. But, a good police officer is always prepared. My mistake! It never happened again in my forty-five-year police career.

That incident reinforced my belief in God and family and made me believe that we all have a destiny in this world. When that gun malfunctioned, it made me feel that God had plans for me. He allowed me to go home with my family. My wife was expecting our daughter and I so much wanted to be there for her and all my children as they grew up and began their lives.

In 1980, I was promoted to sergeant and assigned to the Fourth District, located in the Norwest section of Washington, DC.

Sergeant

The Young Major
1981
Chapter 34

I was working the 6: 00 a.m. to 2:30 p.m. shift. I had just finished roll call and I said it was time to go and get some food. As I walked out the station I see Officers Maurice Williams and Kate Scott. I didn't assign them together, because I knew Maurice and Kate were lazy police officers. Together, you had two nothings and one dead police car. They both had the ability to be good police officers with proper supervision and motivation.

Furthermore, Maurice felt he was a lover and attempted to date every police woman in the police district. I will say one thing for him, he didn't have any children. I never respected a man that had children all over the place and didn't take care of them, especially policemen. We have such a bad reputation with being women beaters, drinkers, bad fathers, and having been married several times. None of those things applied to me. Hell, I had been married a few times, but I always had morals about the way I did things. I was a product of my up-coming.

My parents and grand-parents were my role models. In that Officer William's scout car would not start, I had to assign them together. I was required to have three 10-4 units, which are two police officers assigned to a car. So, the two nothings were going to work together today.

I walked over to Williams and said, "Williams, you and Kate are partners for the remaining of the day."

I could see it in William's eyes. He couldn't wait to get Kate in the vehicle and start begging for a date. This young man wouldn't stop until he was victorious. I knew Kate could handle him. I just wanted them to be better police officers. I said to myself, *I'll monitor them. Hell, we only had four more hours to work.*

As Kate walked over to Williams' scout car, Williams open the door.

The first thing she said, "Boy, I don't want no shit from you today. I will shoot your ass and say it was an accident and you know that I am a better shot than anyone on the department. My last boyfriend had just had such an accident and he still has a limp."

Williams said, "Officer Kate, it is an honor to be acquainted with you for the next few hours."

Kate stated; "Just close the damn door. The dispatcher is asking for units to take assignments."

Williams, "Let's go girl and do some work. Sergeant

Kittrell, you can depend on us Sir and thank you for this opportunity to serve you."

I laughed and just said, "Get me through this day." I had no idea what was about to take place.

Approximately one hour later Officers Williams and Scott received an assignment to check on the welfare of a young lady. When the officers arrived on the scene they were met by Mr. and Ms. Kettering in front of the home of a young lady named Mary who was a major in the US Army. The Kettering's were Mary's Aunt and Uncle. Mr. Kettering informed me that their niece called every day and said, "Hi."

They had not heard from their niece in two days which was not normal for her. Mr. Kettering further stated that they were very close family and his niece was his brother's daughter. Major Kettering was from Florida and didn't like the big city. She had been in the army for approximately 6 years and was 26 years old.

As Mr. Kettering was talking, suddenly his wife started to shake. Mr. Kettering immediately said, "Baby everything is ok. The police are here and they will check the house. Mary probably went out of town and just forgot to tell us."

Ms. Kettering looked at her husband and said, "You know that is not like Mary. She always calls us every day without failure; you know that.

Mr. Kettering looked down at the ground for a second. I told the Kettering's, "Everything that everything will be ok. We will look around the house."

I ask if Mr. Kettering had a key to the house and he said, "Mary changed the locks and she hasn't give us our keys yet. She said there had been several burglaries in the area and she wanted some extra protection."

I knew that burglaries had increased in the area. I didn't want to tell the Kettering's. I didn't want to scare them.

I was on scene because Officers Williams and Scott had called for a supervisor to get permission to break into the house to search the same. They just didn't want to make the decision. Being police officers and with an emergency, they could have entered the house by-way of force. They just were afraid to make the decision. I knew them well and they were not about to rock the boat in any way when it came to making decisions about police work. I could tell when I looked in their eyes; it was a police thing.

I told them, "Okay, this is an emergency. Let's kick in the door."

I didn't want to make them feel too bad. I kick the front door open. Even with two locks on the front door, it was not that difficult. I was also much younger and stronger then.

Once we entered the living room, I could tell something was out of place. There was food on the dining room table, just like someone had just been eating the same. Right then, I knew we had a serious problem.

I told Officer Scott to stay in the living room. Williams and I started searching the down stairs; first the dining room, kitchen, clothes, bathroom and basement. Everything I saw told me that something was wrong. It appeared that time had stopped. I have seen these things before and after so many years and so many cases, you get to know when things are out of place. People live a certain way and when the house is left in a certain condition you know something is out of place. Too many doors not closed, dishes in the sink, and coat on the floor, but the dinner table was the key to letting me know that everything was out of order.

I finally told Scott and Williams to search upstairs. I didn't want Scott to think I didn't trust her. She was always trying to be one of the boys. Right or wrong, I was trying to make her feel better about herself. I stayed in the living room making sure no one could come behind us. Even thou we had search the same, you never know, you can always miss something. I was never so proud, that I couldn't make a mistake. After searching the upstairs bedrooms and closet they came back down stairs.

Williams said, "Sergeant, everything is clean. We didn't see anything. I knew that didn't even sound right to me.

I knew my officers and I felt Major Kettering was in this house or evidence that something had happen. I didn't want to make the officers feel too bad, but I knew them. They were lazy, so I said, "Let's make another check."

As I walked up the stairs, I immediately saw a rug rolled in the corner in the second bedroom. There were three bedrooms and the second was in the middle, so it stood out like a big red ball and it was not looking good. I went to the bedroom and I told the officers to cover the stairs and the hallway. As I got closer, I saw plastic inside the carpet obtruding from the ends. I got down on my knees and touched the carpet and it was to damn hard. I rolled the carpet back just a little. I saw this pretty young face looking at me, as if to say, "Why me? Why me?" I waited a few seconds after checking for signs of life and their being none.

Officer Scott said, "Sergeant, is that a body?"

I waited because I was mad that a young person was dead and mad that these two lazy police officers didn't find the body. I stood up and directed Officer Scott to watch the bedroom. I called for an ambulance and a detective unit to respond, after advising the dispatcher what I had. Officer Williams and I searched the bedrooms again to make sure that the suspects had left. But after seeing the body, I suspected that the suspects had left the crime scene.

My concern was now I had to tell the Ketterings that their niece was dead. I wanted to tell them before the other police units arrived. I walked out the house and by this time several people had started to surround the house. Whenever police stay in an area to long, people will notice you. I walked towards the Ketterings and asked Mr. Kettering if I could talk to him by himself. By this time you could hear the ambulance sirens and Ms. Kettering started to cry.

Mr. Kettering looked at me in the eyes and said, "Sergeant, I am a retired Master Sergeant from the United States Army and I have lived through two wars. Now tell me, is my niece inside and is she okay?"

I immediately looked at the Master Sergeant and said, "Sir, I'm sorry. I found a body that I believe is your niece. Please let the police finish their job and I will keep you informed.

"Thank you, Sergeant," he said. "Now, I must comfort my wife and tell her that our niece is dead."

"Before you tell Ms. Kettering, do you have a picture of your niece?"

Mr. Kettering looked on the table in the living room. There is a picture, taken last week, of her graduation from some military school. I remembered observing the picture.

By this time, the Fourth District Detectives and the ambulance crew had arrived on the scene. I briefed them of the situation and we walked back into the house. I gave the picture to the detectives and they started their work. A short time later, the homicide boys arrived and they took over the case. During the whole time that I was walking in front of the house, I notice these two young men looking at everything, and they looked very concerned. I told the homicide detectives about the two guys. Within the next few hours they were arrested and charged with Major Kettering's murder.

The two suspects were brothers and they had broken into Major Kettering's house two days ago, raped her, and suffocated her to death. After they had killed her they rolled her body into the rug. The detectives later informed me that the suspects tried to say that Major Kettering was attempting to perform some type of sex act and died in the process. There was a new sex act being acted out by many people in the New York area. The suspects claimed that they had found the body with the rope around her neck and no clothes on lying in the plastic on the bedroom floor. There were just too many holes in their story and they kept changing the story.

They confessed into breaking into the house, but they stated they did not kill her. We had recovered so much evidence to indicate their guilt that the suspects made a deal before going to trial. They had left finger prints on the Major's clothes and they couldn't explain why. They both were sentenced to 25 years without parole.

Later in the evening, I talked to Officers Scott and Williams and informed them that they should have found the dead body. They both agreed and apologized. We talked further and left with a better understanding.

It was a good conversation and I could tell by their responses that both officers were very disturbed on their failure to search the house properly. I never assigned the two officers to work together again. Officer Williams later became a detective in the Robbery Branch and did a good job. Officer Scott became a very good sergeant and after working in the narcotic branch. She also was a good wife and mother with three little girls. She named her first daughter Mary, after Major Mary Kettering.

I attended Major Kettering's funeral. It was a very sad funeral. The Kettering family felt they had lost their only daughter. I wore a blue suit. I had learned blue was Major Kettering's favored color. Everyone in the Kettering family recognized me as Sergeant Kittrell which made me feel very good. I attended the whole service.

Approximately 10 years later, suspect #1 was killed by another inmate. Suspect #2 died of AIDS while in prison, 21 years later.

A Lady
1982
Chapter 35

I was working the midnight shift and it was about 1:30 a.m. I had just grabbed a coffee from the Seven 11 and I said *it was a very beautiful night*. As I approached Georgia Avenue and Military Road, I saw a brand-new Cadillac parked to the curb. A young lady was inside, crying. I parked my cruiser and walked towards the vehicle. I knocked on the window. As the young lady rolled down the window, I recognize the driver as a Television celebrity that lived in the rich area of town, upper part of 16TH Street. Her face was bruised and I could tell that someone had struck her several times to the face.

She looked at me and started crying.

I said, "Ms., everything will be okay. Would you like for me to call an ambulance?"

"No, I don't want anyone to see me in this condition."

"I understand," I said. "We have a room at the hospital where you can be treated in private."

"I just want to sit here for a while," the young lady said. "I would like to process what just happen.

"My life is falling apart. My husband is about to leave me. I should be happy, but he is a piece of work. He cheats on me, spends my money, doesn't work, and bosses me around. Now the fucker wants to beat me.

"Well that just isn't going to happen. I have worked too hard to reach this place in my life and I wasn't raised to be abused."

"Sergeant, do you have a cigarette?"

"No ma'am. I don't smoke."

"Good," she said. "They will kill you at the end. Are you married sergeant?

"Yes. I have been married for approximately four years.

"How are things going for you? Are there good days and bad ones, also?

The lady found a cigarette in her vehicle, got gold lighter, and lit the cigarette.

I said, "Ms. Is that real gold?"

"Yes," she said. "A king gave it to me after an interview. The king even asked me to spend the night with him. I said, 'No thank you. Do you want the lighter back?' The King laughed and said, 'I am a gentleman and a king. We don't do such things.' The King use to send flowers to me once a month for year. After that, he gave up. Somebody in his country shot him. He was a very nice man. Chased women, but did a lot for his country."

"Ms., I think I should take you to the hospital."

The lady got in my vehicle. I made sure no one saw her. Even beaten up, the lady was very beautiful. She had two diamond rings on each hand and a gold diamond watch. Her perfume smelled like roses. Even abused, the lady walked to my police vehicle as a lady.

I said to myself, *how a man could beat somebody as beautiful as she was*. As she was seated in my vehicle I could see that the lady was attempting to recover herself. I told her that her vehicle would be ok. I would have other police officers check on the car.

The lady said, "Don't trouble yourself. I brought it for my soon to be ex-husband, last week for a birthday present, and it is in my name. I am going to give it to a charity. That bastard will not drive it again."

Before we started talking, the lady grabbed her phone from her car. This was the first time I saw a portable phone. I said, *Man, what a woman*. She called her lawyer and asked him to meet her at the hospital.

As we were driving towards the hospital, I ask the lady, "What started the argument between you and your husband?"

I learned that sometimes people like to talk about their problems to a police officer. They feel safe and protected with the police.

The lady said, "My husband just came back from a trip to New York City. I was going through his suits and removing items, so she could send them to the cleaners."

I said to myself, *yea, right, women know their husbands; she probably was doing a field search*. As my mother said, *if you look, you shall find.*

The lady said, "I found a letter from my husband's girlfriend stating she had a great time in New York and looked forward to going to the Island. I immediately went to the bathroom where her husband was taking a shower, pulled back the glass door and said, 'Mother-Fucker, I hope your new bitch has money for a lawyer. I'm going to make sure you give me everything back that I gave you.'

Her husband, Bill, said, 'Let's talk about this thing. You have it all wrong.'

'Fuck you and your let's talk about it,' she said. 'I want you out of my house right now.'

"Bill got out the shower, put on a towel, and grabbed me.

"I immediately hit him. I didn't mean too. It just happened. Then that mother-fucker hit me in the face and the fight was on. My project up-bringing came all back to me. I was bad bitch in my other life."

I stop her and said, "Is Bill dead, shot, stabbed, murdered, buried in the back yard, poisoned, or chopped up?"

She started laughing and said, "No, even though that is a good idea."

We both started laughing. The lady continued smoking and said, "All I wanted was man to be good to me. I have had men all over the world try to hit on me, even a president. But, believe it or not I was saving myself. Now, I have been around the barn a few times. Even dated a married man here and there, but I always said I wanted the perfect marriage. I found Bill at a party that my sister was having two years ago. Bill is a good-looking man and a good kisser and not a bad piece of ass. I said, *what the hell, go for it*. I should have married the postal worker. He was easy. He worked all the time and was always tired. That man could sleep and sleep.

"But, in the beginning, Bill was good to me. He always said the right thing, did the right thing, and he made me look good. Bill could take a party and make it so successful with his charm, education, and worldly knowledge. He supported his wife in her endeavors, which means the mother-fucker didn't work.

"People always said, 'Bill is the perfect husband.' He took me to work and picked me up everywhere; the airport, never late, always early, but never late. My mother loved Bill."

I could tell that the lady was about to lose it now. She had that 1000-yard look. It's a look when a person is about to lose all hope of anything. I turned the volume up on the radio because Ray Charles was singing, *Georgia on My Mind.* I told the lady, "Ray Charles is my favor artist."

I asked her, "Who was the most interesting person you ever interview.

She looked at me and said, "You will not believe it, but it was a woman on death row. She had killed her husband. She was only 29 years old.

"I had just started in the business and was working in Alabama on a story covering the women on death row. In Alabama, they don't mess around. They will burn you down there.

"The women's name was Tony. She had planned to kill her husband for the insurance money and for her two lovers. That's right, two lovers, a man and a woman.

"This chick didn't hold back any punches and she was a coldblooded killer. I forgot to mention, she had kill two other husbands. This girl could make Hitler run and hide.

"On the day that she was executed, I spoke with her and she said that she wasn't sorry for nothing she had done. I plan to write a book about it one day.

"They ask Tony if she had any last words to say. Tony said, 'I will see you all in hell one day.' You know a couple people even applauded after they pronounce her dead. That was one bad bitch. If you see her coming in your dreams, please wake up."

We both laughed.

We arrived at the hospital and I took her to the special room that the hospital had reserved for VIP's. By this time, her lawyer had arrived and he asked, "What you want me to do."

The lady asks, "I am covered on all ends, correct?"

"You are covered," he said. "He gets very little."

The lady looked down at the floor, raised her head, looked at the lawyer and said, "Offer the fucker half and make this a quick deal."

I told the lady that I was about to leave and I ask if I could be of further assistance.

She took my hand and said, "Thank you sergeant. I am so glad you found me. I enjoyed talking to you. Have a great life. She then kissed me on my lips. It felt good.

I left the hospital and directed another unit to check on the welfare of Bill, just to make sure he wasn't dead. The officers reported that Bill was okay and he had asked if we have seen his wife. The officers also reported that there were two lawyers at the house talking with Bill. They worked for the lady. Bill was asking the lawyers, "How can these papers be prepared in such a short time and served at such a late hour?"

Several months later, the lady sent me two tickets to see Ray Charles when he was in town and made reservation to have dinner at a famous restaurant in Washington. I wasn't supposed to take these things by-way of police department directives concerning corruption, but I loved Ray Charles.

Ray sang, *Georgia on My Mind,* and dedicated it to me and my wife. That was very nice. But, Ray said, "From the lady to Sergeant Kittrell and his wife." I had a very long drive home.

I never saw the lady again. She did divorce Bill. I read in the paper that she remarried. They are still married today. I am happy for her. She even had two children.

My Girl
1982
Chapter 36

"The world is my throne so why can I not sit upon it."
LT Marco F. Kittrell, MPDC, (ret)

I am working the 6 a.m. to 3 p.m. tour of duty and I was going to breakfast at the church. It was payday and I had some extra money in my check and I just said I was going to buy me a new suit. The dispatcher said that a person is yelling in the apartment at 5916 16Th Street, NW and is asking for some help. Scout car 154 and Scout Car 155 immediately volunteered for the assignment and I advised the dispatcher that I would also assist.

On my arrival, I see that Scout 154 has already arrived and Officer Rodney King is about to enter the building.

I yelled and said, "King wait for me."

We are met at the entrance of the building by several people that live in the building and they all stated that somebody has been yelling, in apartment #302 for the last two minutes, that someone was beating him. We draw our firearms and approach the apartment. By this time, Scout 155 has arrived with Officer Arthur Scanner. I direct Officer Scanner to the rear of the building, just in case someone attempts to jump out the window. I have seen people jump off the third floor and higher. We listened to the door for a few seconds. There is no noise, just a record playing. The song was *My Girl* by the Temptations.

I knocked on the door and shouted, "Police officer, open the door!" No response. I look at King and give him the signal that I am about to kick the door open. I try the door knob and surprisingly, the door is open. Now this is when, as a police officer, you earn your pay. I opened the door and we can see that the apartment has been ransacked.

We yell in the apartment, "Police, is anyone here?"

No response. We entered further into the apartment, very slowly, guns drawn. I am on the left and King is on the right.

We heard a man, crying in the bathroom, saying, "Why did you make me do this?"

We approached very cautiously and with the bathroom covered by Officer King and me, I see this young man sitting on the floor with a knife in his hand, bloody as a stuck pig. It's a sight I will never forget. Another young man is lying in the bathtub with his head laying back and the tub completely engulfed with blood. I directed the suspect to lie down immediately in the bathroom. I wasn't going to tell him that King is covering the other part of the apartment to make sure that there are no other persons in the apartment.

The suspect fell to the floor. I holstered my weapon and placed handcuffs on the suspect. Officer King is still covering as I arrest the suspect. Officer King calls to Officer Scanner and tells him to come inside the apartment. The suspect is still crying and saying "Why you made me kill you, John?" I later learned that the suspect's name was John, also.

Officer Scanner enters the apartment and said, "What the hell did this crazy mother-fucker do?"

I said, "Stand by. Make the notifications."

The officer calls the dispatcher and asks for an ambulance, detectives, and additional units to assist with controlling the crime scene.

Even though I knew that the man in the bathtub was dead, I still check for any signs of life. There were none. The suspect had stabbed the deceased approximately 40 times. There wasn't much left of his body to address.

It was later learned that the suspect and the deceased had an argument and during the dispute the suspect stabbed the deceased as he was taking a bath. The suspect had wanted to get married and the deceased had found another lover. This was the bloodiest crime scene that I have observed during my career as a police officer to date. Both young men had just graduated from college and were working in the medical field.

After processing the crime scene, responding to the homicide Unit, and giving my statements to the homicide detectives, I went back to the police district to take a shower in the station.

My clothes were bloody. Homicide took the clothes and I took a one hour shower. I still couldn't get that odor off me. I was no longer hungry for breakfast either. I left the office at approximately 7:30 p.m.

Once I arrived at my house and as I was sitting in my car in the drive way, I got hungry. It was Friday night and it was my poker night. I wasn't going to miss the game. I left my house and wanted a steak and potato dinner. I went to the steak house in my area. As I was eating, I kept thinking about the suspect as he was giving his statement at the homicide office. This was a young educated man who had a promising future in front of him. I couldn't understand how a man could result to so much violence, and stab another person with so much rage, just because he wanted somebody else. I have nothing against gay people, but this was not the first time that I had observed so much violence in the gay community, concerning relationships when they go bad.

I recalled back in 1978 when two women broke into another woman's home who had been involved with one of the suspects as her lover.

The suspects held the women down on the floor and pressed a hot iron on the women's face saying, "If you will not have me, no one will want you with this scar on your face."

I arrested those two women and they were both sentenced to 20 years for burglary, kidnapping, and mayhem.

I thought about another case back in 1976. I had arrested a young man named David for stabbing his lover, Mike, in the chest, as he attempted to get into his vehicle. The two men had been arguing and fighting in the street, because Mike was offered a job in Hollywood in a motion picture and he wasn't going to take his lover, David.

I am not saying because they were gay they were violent; I just recalled the cases as I was eating dinner. I said *it takes all kinds of people in the world to make it work*.

Before leaving the restaurant, I saw two men sitting in a booth, eating, and they kissed. They looked like they cared for each other. I said to myself, *I wish them luck*.

God is the judge of people and not me. I have seen people do much worst who weren't gay. These people just happened to be gay.

I got back into my car and when I started the car up, the first song on the radio was *My Girl* by the Temptations. I said a prayer for both Johns. You can't keep this stuff in your head. If you do, you can't do your job and I have a long way to go before retirement.

I stopped and got some gas and there were two women in a vehicle at the station arguing in a vehicle. I could tell by the conversation that they were breaking up, but one of the women didn't agree. I said, *please God let me get to my poker game.* The women stopped arguing, kissed, and as I exited the vehicle, the other women said, "You will always be my friend and my girl.

If I could have related the words to *My Girl* to some numbers, I would have bet the house on it.

I arrived at the poker game and as I entered the house the song playing was, *My Girl* by the Temptations.

What a day!

The Little Girl
Chapter 37

> "What do I see when I consider your eyes, is it me looking at me."
> LT Marco F. Kittrell, MPDC, (ret)

It was a Friday night and I had been watching my little girl all day. I was kind of tired, but I could get through the night. After roll call, I went right to the Seven 11 for some of that good coffee. As I enter the store I said, "Hi." to Melvin. He was a young black kid who was going to school during the day, Howard University. He always wore a Howard shirt. Melvin was very proud to be putting himself through school. He wanted to be a doctor. Melvin was about 19 years old.

When I walked into the store he always stated, "What up, sergeant?" with a smile. He also was tired from studying all day and attending school, but he was determined to be a doctor. Melvin immediately stated, "Sergeant, let me get your coffee tonight."

I said, "Thanks Melvin."

"Sergeant, you look like you're tired. Did you watch your baby and she kept you up?"

I said, "Yes sir. My baby is getting older now, 9 months. She didn't sleep much now. I might need to get a baby sitter."

Melvin immediately stated, "For $50 bucks a day, I'll watch your little girl while you sleep. But, sergeant you must bring her to me and bring plenty of diapers, food, and milk. That isn't included in the price for babysitting.

I smiled and said, "That's ok, Melvin. I going to watch her for four more months and then I will get a baby sitter, a real one. Besides, you are in school during the day."

"Sergeant, if those Jamaicans can work five jobs, so can I.

"Man," I said. "I don't know how they do it. I get tired from just watching them."

"Ok, Sergeant. That coffee is one dollar plus my tip." I smile and paid for my coffee. "Hey Sergeant, no donuts tonight?"

"No sir. I'm going to cut back," I said.

As skinny as you are, you need some food. Hang in their sergeant and be safe. You know those mothers are out there tonight."

I walked to my car and I looked up at the sky. It was such a bright night, very warm, no traffic, and no noise.

I said, *Man, it might be a quiet night tonight.*

The Little Girl 1982

As I started to drink my coffee, I saw this little girl running towards me in the parking lot. I couldn't believe what I saw. The little girl was bleeding around her legs and she had no clothes on. I immediately grabbed a blanket out of the cruiser and threw the same around her. The little girl was shaking and looked right into my eyes and said, "Sergeant, please get my mommy out the trunk." She was very calm and not crying. I recognized that she might be in shock.

I said, "Okay baby. Where is your mommy?"

"By the railroad tracks."

I call the dispatcher and requested an ambulance and some back up. This little girl kept looking in my eyes and I couldn't stop looking at her. All I could see is my little girl. The whole time, I am thinking, *who could hurt such a small child.* By it not being a busy night, the ambulance arrived very quickly.

The ambulance crew was a female and a male. I was glad to see the women, for the child. As the ambulance crew was working on the little girl, I finally asked her name.

She stated, "Get my mommy out the trunk. My name is Nadine."

I said, "Okay Nadine, now where is your mommy?"

I already advise the dispatcher and the police units who were searching the area. I knew that she couldn't have run too far and we were not too far from some railroad tracks. I started questioning Nadine further; color of the vehicle, her mother's name. Nadine started crying and again stated, "Get my mother out of the trunk."

I hugged Nadine as if she was my own daughter. Nadine hugged me back. It was at that time a unit radio a call in and stated, "Be advised, we have located a vehicle fitting the description at 2010 Railroad Avenue." This was only four blocks away.

I got in my car and told the ambulance driver to follow me. Nadine kept looking in my eyes. As we drove off, Nadine looked out the back window of the ambulance with a look I can't get out of my head.

It was a look that said she depended on me to find her mother.

As we were driving to the scene I said, *God please let Nadine's mom be okay*. I talk to God a lot when these things happen. After so many murders, rapes, stabbings, and shootings, I just knew that there was a God and he was in control of the situation. Sometimes, I thought he wasn't listening in that I only talk to him when these types of things occurred. On some occasions things turn out okay and others not so good. I would say, *big guy, give me this one*.

I felt I was due a favor in that we found the young Major dead last week. I started hitting the steering wheel and repeatedly said, "God, you owe me one!"

The Little Girl 1982

When we arrived at the railroad tracks, there was only one light on and three policemen looking down at the ground. At that time, I knew Nadine's mom was here. As I exited my vehicle, I looked back at the ambulance and Nadine was saying through the window, "Get my mommy out of the trunk." I couldn't hear her, but I could read her words as she moved her mouth. For some reason, I grabbed that coffee. I don't know why. Maybe I felt it would help as I knew what I was about to see.

It was like a horror movie. No one was talking, no noise, and a very bright night with only one light on over the vehicle. As I walked towards the vehicle I said, "God, please let Nadine's mom be alive. Give me this one now. You owe me one. It has been a bad month."

Officer Dickerson said, "Sergeant, she is in the trunk." He never looked at me. I did see a tear, just one. Officer Dickerson also had a daughter, born just two days ago.

It was very strange. All the police officers on the scene were experience officers and had been exposed to numerous incidents of this nature, but in this case, they all just kept looking down at the ground.

I walked toward the car and I saw what appeared to be Nadine's mom's arm hanging out from the trunk. As I considered the trunk, I saw the wide-open eyes looking at me. Before I checked any vital signs, I knew she was dead. I later learned that Nadine's mom's name was Ms. Marie Karen Anderson.

Ms. Anderson was wearing a white summer dress, short to her knees. She had long black hair and Nadine look just like her. Her throat had been cut and they did a very bad job. Her dress was soaked in blood and torn in several places. Even though Ms. Anderson's face was bruised and both eyes swollen, I could tell she was very beautiful.

You could tell she had battled them and she must have put up one damn good fight. Several of Ms. Anderson's her nails were broken off and her hair was in such a way I could tell that the suspects had pulled her hair several times. With many years on the job, you pick up these things. Ms. Anderson was still wearing her white pearl ear rings and white pearl necklace. As I continued looking at Ms. Anderson, I felt as if she was asking me, "Is my little girl ok?"

By this time, the ambulance crew came over to the vehicle and verified that Ms. Anderson was dead. I could tell that she had been raped and beaten.

I walked back to the ambulance to be with Nadine. The Homicide Unit had arrived on the scene and these guys were good policemen, the old fashion kind. They felt something for the people in the city. Detectives Michael Jenkins and Ron Brown, both with 20 plus years on the job. I have worked many cases with them over the years. They knew what they were doing. They both wore glasses. They had been working together so long that they even looked alike except Detective Jenkins was black and Detective Brown was white. They also had that homicide look, as I called it.

They looked right through you and listened very closely to everything you said. Before I could brief the detectives, they already had most of the information. They even informed me of some things that I was not aware off. Mr. Anderson had reported his wife missing and described her vehicle. By now the information was already compiled and the homicide boys were informed that an unknown person had called the police and informed them of the attack.

Detective Johnson, homicide, arrived on the scene with a young man in the back of the vehicle. I could tell he must have been Ms. Anderson's husband. He had that look. As a policeman it doesn't take too long to place people in the rights holes. I recognized Nadine's eyes. Detectives Jenkins and Brown further stated that they had located a witness to the incident and the witness was being interviewed. At times like this, a good officer never gives too much information until they have all the facts, even to another policeman. So, I knew why he said, "A witness," the entire time. Nadine kept looking at me through the window in the ambulance. Those eyes, I will never forget.

Detective Jenkins walked over to Ms. Anderson's vehicle and furthered his investigation. I walk with Detective Brown. He said, "Okay sergeant, follow me." Even though I was a sergeant, the Homicide Detectives were in charge and they acted like they were in charge.

As we approached Detective Johnson's vehicle, Mr. Anderson jumped out the rear of the vehicle. Detective Brown grabbed him and said, "I understand, Mr. Anderson," as he was crying profusely.

Mr. Anderson kept saying, "Is that my wife? Is that my wife? Where is my little girl?"

Nadine saw her father and said with a very loud voice, only once "Daddy!"

We took Mr. Anderson over to Nadine and they both hugged each other very hard, Mr. Anderson picked his daughter up and said, "Daddy is here. Daddy is here."

I could only think of my little girl.

Nadine kept saying, "Daddy, Get mommy out the trunk."

Detective Jenkins looked at Detective Brown and gave him the look as if to say, *it is time to identify the body*. Detective Brown took Mr. Anderson to the side, as I stood next to Nadine. The detective said, "Mr. Anderson, prepare yourself and let's go over to the car. You must identify your wife."

Mr. Anderson stopped crying, looked at the detective and said, "I am ready."

I stayed with Nadine. She couldn't see anything. Nadine started shaking. I felt so helpless.

The female ambulance driver, Officer Mary Smith said, "Sergeant, let me have her." I didn't want to let Nadine go because she kept holding on me. Officer Smith said, "I got you, baby." Nadine continued to look at me in my eyes, and those eyes are still with me today.

Mr. Anderson reached his wife and he fell to the ground with his hands in the air saying, "God, why me? Why me? God, why me? My wife is gone, my wife is gone. What have those mother-fuckers done to my wife, my pretty wife?"

Both detectives grabbed Mr. Anderson and held him. Nothing else was said. The other police officers on the scene never looked at Mr. Anderson, only at the ground. I never understood that. In most cases police love to stare at people during times of hardship.

I walked back to the ambulance as they were in the process of driving Nadine to the hospital. Nadine's aunt, Ms Anderson's twin sister, who was a nurse, had arrived on the scene and she was with Nadine. As the ambulance drove away, Nadine looks through that small window staring at me.

I get back in my cruiser. The police technicians are processing the crime scene. I drive back to the 7-11, park in the parking lot, and start drinking that cold coffee, I cried like I never had before in my life. All I could think is *how a human being could do such a thing to another person?*

That little girl is now without a mother. A husband has lost his wife. Somebody's child is dead and some human is no more. I cried for about three minutes and I just stopped. I said, *this isn't the first murder I have seen and it will not be the last.*

Melvin was looking at me through the window, but didn't say anything. He brought me another cup of coffee and said, "Sergeant, this is on me."

I didn't say anything. I don't know why. I think I was ashamed because this young man saw me crying.

Melvin stated, "Sergeant, I never knew my father. I saw a picture of him once. But, you know, if I had a father, I wish he was like you. You are a good man who gives a damn."

"I heard some other policeman talking about that little girl when they were in the store getting their free coffee and donuts. You know Sergeant; you are the only police officer that pays for the coffee. Sergeant for the next two weeks the coffee is on me and I am going to start charging those other cheap deadbeats."

We both started laughing. I said, "I will see you, Melvin."

"Until tomorrow Sergeant."

Before I left the parking lot, I notice that Melvin had a bad limp. I have been drinking this kid's coffee for 12 months and I have just notice that he had a bad leg, and I thought I was good police man. I started laughing again.

Before I could get back to the Police District, Detective Johnson called me over the police radio and asked if he could meet me somewhere on the street. I meet him two blocks from the 7-11.

The Little Girl 1982

Detective Johnson told me, "Good news, we caught those suspects."

He went on to explain what happen. Ms. Anderson had picked her daughter up from the baby sitter's house only three blocks away from the crime scene. The four suspects saw Ms. Anderson placing Nadine in the back seat of her car. As Ms. Anderson was about to open her front door, they grabbed her and drove her vehicle to the railroad tracks. There they beat Ms. Anderson and raped her and attempted to rape her daughter. The witness said that she fought the suspects like a man and told her daughter to run and Nadine did. The little girl hides in the woods and watched her mother being attacked.

Nadine was about to go back to her mother and attempt to help, but the witness stopped her and told her to run.

You will never believe who the witness was. It was a homeless person that lived in the woods.

His name was Ralph Wilkins. Ralph told the little girl to go to the 7-11, because there is a sergeant that gets his free coffee every night around this time. His name is Sergeant Kittrell and you can trust him. Now I know why Nadine kept looking at me.

Detective Johnson further stated that the suspects stole Ms. Anderson's credit cards and used one to purchase gas. The homicide detective reviewed the gas station's video tapes. Detectives Jenkins and Brown recognized one of the suspects as a local drug user. We figured they went to 14Th and U Street to cop some drugs. Detectives Jenkins and Brown had their local snitches be on the look-out for the suspects. Twenty minutes later, one of the local snitches called. All four suspects were located and arrested. We got confessions, evidence, and a good witness, but Ralph was beating himself up because he couldn't help Ms. Anderson.

I said, "Ralph saved Nadine's' life and helped capture the four mother-fuckers that committed the crime."

"Sergeant, I just thought I'd let you know," said the detective, "Good job, Sergeant."

I said, "No. You guys are damn good policeman. Great job! You made my day. How is Nadine?"

"Not to good. When they told her that her mother was dead she just fainted.

I asked, "How old was Nadine?"

"She was 11 years and her mother was 31 years old. Nadine has a very large family. They are all at the hospital. It will take a long time, but time resolves everything, maybe. All right, sergeant, go home and kiss your little girl. Also, sergeant, stay off that 7-11 coffee. Look at me. I use to be a good looking black guy, now I am a fat white man."

We both laughed. Detective Johnson pointed at me and drove off with his tongue out laughing. That was the end of my shift.

I told God, "You still owe me one, but thanks for having those four-people arrested.

I guess God said, "You are welcome."

I always thought God and I had a special relationship. He has saved me too many times. When I got home, I kissed my daughter and put her in bed with my wife and me as we slept.

Even now, I look at all the girls in my family with the need for safety. All our children are special to us. Keep them close and tell them every day, how much you love them.

Sergeant James Frank
1982
Chapter 38

It is Monday night and I am working the 12 a.m. to 8 a.m. shift; the deadly midnights. The captain walked into the sergeant's office and said, "Great job. The promotion list is out. You are high on the lieutenant list and you probably will be promoted to lieutenant very soon."

I said, "Thank you captain, and thanks for the motivation."

He replied, "Good job, Kittrell. You were a good sergeant and you should make a good lieutenant."

"Effective immediately, you are acting lieutenant for the midnight shift until you get promoted," and he walked out the office. After 9 years on the police force, I learned one thing. Bullshit goes a long way. The captain and I were never friends and he never motivated me. I just said that to make him feel good. I didn't want to burn my bridges. The captain was going to be around for a while. It was rumored that the Chief of

Police was thinking about promoting that old trash can, so you never know. I will say one thing about him. He never rocked the boat, he knew how the game was played, and he played it very well; too well.

I wasn't crazy about being on midnights again, especially with these wild police officers. I walked outside to get in my cruiser to start the tour and I see Sergeant James Frank pumping gas into his police cruiser. Sergeant Frank is talking to himself, his shirt is bloody and his face is red as a fire truck. The sergeant's hair, what is left of it, looked like Don King's, the fight promoter. His pants were dirty and his right eye was bloody. Also, the sergeant had a shotgun in the front seat of his police cruiser. This did not look good to me.

Sergeant Frank was one of the sergeants, when I first join the police force, to take me under his wing and teach me how to be a police officer and perhaps a supervisor. Sergeant Frank was very kind to me and acted like he wanted me to be something. So, I was very concern how I was going to talk to the old sergeant.

Sergeant Frank was 64 years old. After sixty, a police officer on the WMPD must get approval to stay on the force. Every year the sergeant got his approval. Hell, he knew everybody on Capitol Hill and in the DC Government and the community loved him. It wasn't hard to do. Sergeant Frank was also attached to the Presidential detail, the officers that escort the President of the Unite States through the City of Washington. Hell, the sergeant has been doing that for 40 years. He had a picture of him with every President he escorted and their family. Sergeant Frank and the current President rode horses together, once a month.

The sergeant had the juice. The police department needed money for their budget last year and the Chief of Police called Sergeant Frank for help and the police department got the money. I also liked the sergeant and respected him, but I couldn't let him go hunting for a suspect in the condition that he was in. I respected him, so I don't want to disrespect the old sergeant.

I walked over to Sergeant Frank and said, "What's up, sergeant?"

"Hi, Kittrell, I don't have much time to talk. I am going hunting for a mother-fucker."

"Sergeant, can you tell me what happened?" I asked.

"Don't you see how I look?" he said. "Can't you tell that something happened? I don't have time to explain what happened. I am going hunting for a mother fucker."

I replied, "Now sergeant, can we please slow down for just a few moments? Can you please tell me what happen?"

I was at 16Th and Lamont Street, NW. I told this guy to get off the corner. We had several complaints about people hanging on the corner. The son of bitch was only 5 feet tall, if that. This mother-fucker told me that, 'if I was not wearing that badge, he would place his foot up my ass.'

"Now this was just not going to happen. I've been a policeman for 40 years, plus, and no mother-fucker is going to place his foot up my ass. I walked over to this little punk and he hit me in my face with a rock. I didn't see that damn rock in his hand. He knocked me down to the fucking ground. I would have shot the bastard, but the little fucker ran."

So, why didn't you call for backup?" I asked.

"I don't need a damn back up! I can handle any and everything that comes near me. The little fucker just caught me off guard. I going to find that mother-fucker, kick his ass, hit him with a rock, arrest him, and then bring that little mother-fucker in."

By this time, I know that the sergeant is showing his age by not thinking the problem through. I didn't want to be an accessory to a murder; the sergeant's murder by this little mother-fucker, if the sergeant found him. Even though Sergeant Frank was talking crazy and he was totally wrong, I didn't want to hurt him. He was a good man and always took care of me when I was a young police officer and police cadet. Being policemen, you should not allow your personal feelings to get in the way of your decision making, but sometimes it is very hard. In my case, I wanted to treat the sergeant gently like my father, but I had to do my job.

I said, "Sergeant, you know that I am now the acting lieutenant on the midnight shift."

Sergeant Frank looked at me. "Great fucking job! I hope you don't turn into one of these sorry mother-fuckers who call themselves managers."

"No Sergeant, you taught me well."

"Good! Now get the fucking out my way. I'm going man hunting for a bad ass.

I looked at him. "Sergeant, you are hurt and you need some medical attention. We can get this mother-fucker, after you get some attention."

"I don't need no damn doctor! What are you, a little girl? This is a street thing and the streets are always looking at you. I told you that seven years ago. You must have forgotten where you came from."

"No sir," I said, "I haven't, but this isn't right and someone is going to get hurt and maybe it might just be you."

"I'm sorry, Lieutenant Kittrell, I know that the police department comes first and not its men."

That was the first time somebody called me Lieutenant and it felt good. I also remembered what Sergeant Frank told me seven years ago.

He said, "Kittrell, no matter what happens on this job, one day you will need to decide something concerning someone you love, respect, and care for on this job. Do the right thing, because in the morning the boys down town will look at you and go over your decision with a fine tooth comb. So, do the best you can and be satisfied with yourself, no matter who it might hurt. They might not like it, but they will respect you." That was exactly what I was about to do.

"Sergeant Frank, I give you a direct order to park your cruiser on this parking lot, go into my office and wait for the ambulance crew to treat you, and wait for the police detective, who will interview you. You will give them an exact account of what took place today concerning that mother-fucker that struck you with the rock. Is that clear, sergeant?"

Sergeant Frank looked at me and said, "Mother-fucker, I can't believe you, and you are giving me," as he points his finger to his chest, "a direct order. Mother-fucker and mother-fucker! People just don't remember any got-damn thing. Mother-fucker!"

Sergeant Frank got in his cruiser, parks the same, and followed my orders. As he walked towards my office, the sergeant starts smoking (He was a chain smoker), stops at the door, turns around, looks at me and says, "Mother-fucker, I can't believe Kittrell, he gave me a direct order. Mother-fucker!"

The next day when I entered my office, I saw a bottle of Hennessey, a box of doughnuts, and a large 7-11 coffee on my desk, along with a card. I open the same and it was from Sergeant Frank.

It said, "Thanks for being there. You really have grown and I am proud of you, Lieutenant Kittrell."

It was signed, "From a fat old white man. Motherfucker, I think it is time for me to retire."

The detectives located a witness that observed the assault on Sergeant Frank. The suspect was located, arrested, and served 12 months in jail.

Sergeant Frank retired 12 months later and it was one of the biggest parties that the police department ever had. The hotel was sold out. I never saw so many politicians in one room, except at an inaugural of a president.

Several Chiefs of Police that had retired in the last forty years were there. I even cried a little, when he gave his speech. He reminded me of that sergeant that I met 10 years earlier.

Sergeant Frank's grandson joined the police department that same year and he worked for me for a year. I kept an eye on the young man. He was a good police officer.

Sergeant Frank died the next year. He had cancer and a very large funeral. I cried.

Lieutenant

I was promoted to the rank of lieutenant in 1982

The Armed Robbery Gone Bad 1992
Chapter 39

It was approximately 7:30 p.m. and I was driving on South Capitol Street, S.E. It was a very quiet night and nothing much was going on. It was about that time when the dispatcher stated that an armed robbery was in progress and shots had been fired. I was only three blocks away from the store. I advised the dispatcher that I would respond.

On my arrival, I saw a man in the door way that I recognized as Chin Lee. He was the owner and I had eaten there often. By this time several other police units were arriving on the scene. Mr. Lee stated that he had just been robbed and the robber had fired several shots at him.

I ask if he or any one had been injured.

Mr. Lee said. "No, but the Mother-Fucker couldn't have gotten too far."

His English wasn't that good so he sounded very funny when he cursed. I hadn't heard Mr. Lee curse before. I used to love talking to Mr. Lee, because he had a very proud history concerning his family. He also loved America very much. He always stated that he left his country a very poor man, but this country allowed him and his brothers to start businesses and they were all doing very well.

Mr. Lee also always stated that men who must curse to express themselves are men that have no vision in communicating with others and would fail in their dreams of achieving any goals in life. "A man must resort to using such shallow words, is a man that has no future." For this reason, I was shocked when he used the word mother-fucker. I even smiled.

I looked on the ground and saw a trace of blood.

I asked Mr. Lee, "Did you injure the suspect?"

Mr. Lee said, "You damn right I did. I tried to chop his fuckin hand off. Follow me and I'll show you, lieutenant."

By this time, the other units had started canvassing the area for the suspect as Mr. Lee and his family had given us a description.

When I entered the store, I couldn't believe my eyes. I saw a hand imbedded in the counter with a gun still attached to the hand and a meat cleaver also attach to the same.

"What the hell happen, Mr. Lee?"

"Lieutenant, that mother-fucker entered my store and

pointed a gun at my family and said, 'Give me the fuckin money or I will killed you all.' I gave him some money and asked him not to hurt my family.

"After the mother-fucker took the money from me, he turned his head for a second and that was all the time that I needed. I took my favorite meat cleaver, which I had place under the counter, and chopped his fuckin hand completely off, with the gun still in its grip. That was when the gun started firing downward into the counter by itself. The mother-fucker then ran out the store like the coward that he was. He will not be pointing guns with that hand anymore, the mother-fucker!"

The suspect was later captured only three blocks away from the store and he was missing a hand.

Even though a robbery just occurred, business is business, and Mr. Lee asked if any of the police officers were hungry.

Mr. Lee was famous for his food on the police force.

Nobody ordered food that day.

Officer James Brooks
1992
Chapter 40

    I was leaving the Police District at approximately 11:30 p.m. after working a 9-hour shift. I'd had a hard day. I was assigned to the Vice Unit as the Commander. As I am exiting from the back door, I see Officer James Brooks. He was a young officer, very aggressive, and was always trying to improve himself. I really liked the officer, but I use to tell him, "Stop taking too many high risks."

    He was a go getter and very loyal to his profession. I just didn't like the idea that he took so many chances when it came to making arrests. Officer Brooks was also getting off duty. He was still working in the patrol section as a patrol officer. He was doing a good job, just took too many unnecessary risks.

    He told me to have a good night and he was about to go home. His wife was in their vehicle with their three children, two boys and one little girl. I told officer Brooks to see me tomorrow, because I still had his personal note book that he had left in my police cruiser.

Two days before, I had recruited him and other young police officers in the patrol section to help me and my drug unit in executing some search warrants for illegal drugs. I used to allow the young officers to work on some drug cases that my unit was investigating when it came down to executing these types of warrants.

It allowed me to evaluate future officers that wanted to work in the narcotic unit. It also gave the young officers a chance to work out of uniform; it was a good morale motivator. Brooks was young and a very fast runner. If the suspects would jump out the windows, I knew Brooks could catch them. He had a good eye for suspects attempting to throw away illegal drugs when the suspects exited the apartments. I also liked Brooks and I wanted to make him a better officer, if I could. I had seen a great improvement in the officer's attitude when addressing police issues and problems.

At one time, Brooks worked for me when I was a Lieutenant in the patrol section. The officer had three years on the job at the time. On many assignments, Brooks would handle the calls and not wait for his back up. I even disciplined him once for failing to follow proper police procedures. I felt this was in the best interest, for not only the officer, but the police department as well. As a supervisor, if you allow a subordinate to constantly violate police procedures and something goes wrong, the supervisor and the department is held liable. My main concern was that I had learned over the years that when a police officer is killed, injured, or goes bad (such as police corruption cases), some supervisors could have stopped the officer at an early stage in the officer's career. That would have prevented the incident. This in no way takes away from the brave acts of police officers that have died in the line of duty. I just know that in so many cases where police officers have been killed or injured in the line of duty, the officers failed to follow some established procedures or were just allowed to continue with bad habits as a police officer.

As the old saying goes, "One day it is okay, but the next day you are wrong." As policemen, you must constantly make decisions concerning people, most of them are judgmental. The majority of the decisions are good ones, but when one goes bad, the whole world knows.

When I was young, I thought, *this was wrong*. As I got older, I realized that policemen have such a great responsibility and duty to the community that whoever made that rule was correct. A police officer can arrest you, seize your property, execute search and arrest warrants, tell you to stop and go, and even take your life. This duty can be performed by only the best society can offer and you must be able to handle such a responsibility. To bear this burden is a monumental task. This reflection shapes my thinking when dealing with young police officers. What you do today will be with them the rest of their lives.

I recalled once when officer Brooks chased a suspect into an abandon apartment. The suspect was wanted for robbery. I didn't like how the incident started. For months earlier we were looking for a wanted suspect name Little Man. He had committed several robberies in the area and on three occasions he shot three different people. A witness identified Little Man and told us, the police, where he resided. The police stationed several police officers at look-out posts in the area were Little Man lived to keep Little Man contained. The police officers were given precise directions to keep Little Man under surveillance and not take any actions until directed. We knew that Little Man was very dangerous and didn't want to go back to jail. Our plan was to take Little Man as he was leaving his house and about to enter his vehicle, where very few citizens were present.

Little Man always parked his vehicle in a secure and secluded location. The plan that we had prepared was a good one.

Officer Brook, who was stationed at a look-out post, was also given the same proper instructions on how we were going to execute the plan.

As my luck would have it, Little Man exited his apartment and started walking towards Officer Brooks. All the police officers assigned to look-out posts were in civilian attire and they blended in the area quit well. Another officer was watching Officer Brooks. The area was very well secured for all the officers involved in the operation.

As Little Man approached, Officer Brooks, for no apparent reason, drew is firearm and directed Little Man to stop and place his hands over his head. Little Man, being a street wise criminal, he knew that the police weren't going to kill him under the present conditions.

Criminal are not stupid. Most of them know the law better than the police officer. Even though, Little Man had killed someone and Officer Brooks would have been legal in shooting Little Man, Little Man probably felt the officer would not shoot him with so many people in the immediately area. In that Officer Brooks initiated the incident, the officer placed several people lives in jeopardy. If Brook would have waited until Little Man had reached his vehicle, there would have been no bystanders in the area and we could have captured Little Man without harm to the citizens in the area. Little Man took off running. Now we had a big problem.

A man who had committed several robberies, killed two people, and shot another person was on the run and probably armed. A lot of people in the immediately danger area could be hurt, all because a police officer failed to follow directions.

All the other police officers gave chase. Everyone had their firearms out; people were yelling, and all I could see were little children running. I said, *Oh God, let us get this so and so before someone gets killed.*

By this time Little Man drew his weapon. I thought it was the biggest gun in the world. Everything was going real fast, too fast. Little Man ran into an apartment building with

Officer Brooks right behind him. Within seconds I heard two-gun shots. I could tell they were from two different guns.

I said, *Mother-Fucker, I hope this officer isn't dead, because I wanted to shoot him myself for getting this whole mess started.* I was the first to reach Brooks. Brooks had shot and kill Little Man after Little Man attempted to shoot Officer Brooks.

It was a very small hallway. No bigger than 5x5. Brooks was standing over Little Man with his service weapon in hand. The gun was still smoking. Little Man had his gun in his hand, eyes wide open looking at Officer Brooks, with a big bullet hole in his chest. I was mad at Officer Brooks for initiating the incident and now I had to deal with a police shooting; my officer had just killed someone.

The majority of police officers are good people and wouldn't discharge their weapon until they had thought the matter through and had no other recourse but to discharge their weapon. This also applied to Officer Brooks. He was very aggressive, but not a bad officer. I just wanted the officer to be a better team player, be patient, and think the problem through before reacting. In police work things happen fast, but as a police officer you still have time to think and make good decisions. In the majority of the cases that is the different between a professional police officer and a non-professional. They think before they react. Criminals also recognize this characteristic in policemen. Most criminals think through the problem when addressing situations. Criminals that make their living by committing crimes are good judge of character and read people very well, too well. That is their trade and they want to be recognized for the same.

I myself had been in two police shootings resulting in the death of two people. I know how it affected me, so I could relate to Officer Brooks' possible reaction to the shooting.

I asked Officer Brooks "Are you ok?"

The Officer replied, "Lieutenant, I don't know why Little Man would try to shoot me."

I told the officer, "Little Man is a professional criminal and you were between him and freedom. Little Man had no problem in shooting you or anybody else if that allowed him to be free and not in jail."

Officer Brooks looked at Little Man and said, "You are right, LT. I had no other choice."

I grabbed the officer by the neck. "You remember that. You had no other choice. It means you get to go home tonight to your family and kiss your wife and two boys. That is what matters. Life is too short and on this job, it is even shorter."

The officer looked at me and said, "Thanks LT. I really love my family."

I wanted to tell Officer Brooks, if he would have followed my directions, maybe it would have turn out differently. I believe that the incident would had still resulted in a shooting and probably the death of Little Man, but under my conditions and controlled by the police with every officer going home to their families and love ones. I had planned to tell this to Officer Brooks, but this was not the time.

I saw a pregnant woman running towards the scene crying profusely and saying, "They shot little Man."

Two police officers grabbed her and stopped her from running into the apartment. I recognize the young lady as Little Man's girlfriend. During the investigation, we learned her name was Kari. As the police officers were talking to Kari, she became extremely upset and very uncontrollable. Detective Gilmore, a Seventh District Detective who had arrived on the scene, started to talk with her and told the officers that he would handle it. I knew Detective Gilmore. He was a good detective and very experience in handling such matters. The detective always could handle people who had just lost a love one. He was good at it and he knew it. He was like an opera singer performing. No other person could interview people the way Detective Gilmore could. Within thirty minutes he had Kari back at the police station, giving a statement and providing more information on little Man's criminal activities. I was later informed by the detective that Little Man had committed a robbery in Maryland and shot someone two days ago. Like I said Detective Gilmore was like an opera singer, good at his craft.

Other officers arrived on the scene and we began the task of processing the crime scene, recovering evidence, and locating witnesses. In this neighborhood, I knew what to expect right away; nothing. But based on prior experience I knew someone will always call later and want to meet you somewhere and tell you everything. There were a lot good people in the area, but could not get too involved because they were surrounded by too many people who didn't like the police and wanted everyone to feel the same. That was a shame, because as a police officer I had worked in this community and knew the people. They were good people. Drugs had taken down the neighborhood. The crack dilemma was at its worst in this neighborhood. The drug gangs had taken over the neighborhood with shootings, killings, stabbings, and prostitution of the young girls and boys.

I worked this area approximately 6 years ago as a police officer. It was your average neighbor with good people making a good living. I can't remember receiving many police calls for service in the area during those times. The area consisted of married people with children, grandparents, and just good people. Throughout the year children played football, baseball, tennis, and even a golf league was established. I really enjoyed the people. During the summer, someone was always having a cookout and the police ate very well.

Once the drug gangs moved in, most of the good people that could get out did. Many people were stuck because of their financial situation. The police worked very hard to address the drug gangs by making arrests, executing search and arrest warrants, and establishing a police substation. Police officers worked out of a police trailer. It made the citizens feel good that the police were there. The problem was so big it would take a combined effort of the United States, District of Columbia Government, and citizens to resolve the drug gangs. I knew in time the citizens would have their neighborhood back.

My captain wanted me to recommend Officer Brooks for a commendation. I talked the captain out of the recommendation. After he heard my reasons, he accepted the same and told me to handle the matter. Officer Brooks was off duty for approximately 60 days. It took that long to get the case through the Grand Jury and adjudicate the matter. Whenever police officers are involved in the death of a person, the case is referred to a Grand Jury for their decision to either prosecute the officer or not. In a majority of the cases there is no problem, but officers have been charges. Officer Brooks was cleared of any wrong doing and reported back to duty.

On the officer's return to work, the other police officers treated him like he was a hero. I never agreed with that type of reaction when a police officer took someone's life. I felt that we should have been better than that, but that was the way it was back in those days. The department offered counseling services for the officer and his family, because a police officer's family also goes through changes when their spouse or love ones have been in an incident of this magnitude.

Officer Brooks and I talked about two hours concerning the shooting. I wanted to get my point across but still not damage the young officer. We had a good discussion and I felt Officer Brooks took my recommendations and counseling very well. I believe I can read people very well, especially police officer. I felt good after the conversation.

I didn't want the officer to think that what happened was the correct course of action. It wasn't and the officer or other people could have been hurt or killed. Like I said, Little Man would have probably been shot and died at the scene anyway, but under our control and no other person would have possibly been hurt.

Officer Brooks got into his vehicle with his family and drove off. Before I could get to my vehicle, I remembered that I had left something in my office. I returned to my office, retrieved the paperwork, and returned to the parking lot to enter my vehicle.

I heard police vehicles going past the police district with their sirens blasting. I also saw police officers running out the building and getting in their police cruisers and exiting the parking lot with extreme urgency. I knew that a police officer had been possibly shot, because police only act like this when a police officer has been seriously injured. No matter what the police do to each other, when it comes down to helping a fellow officer during times of emergency, there is nothing like it. All police officers know that it could be them next and when you need help, seconds are critical. I know. I have been there. I ran back to the building and asked Sergeant Alvin Price, as he is about to get into his vehicle, who has been injured.

The sergeant says, "Officer Brooks has been shot and he is unconscious. He was shot by another police officer. Lieutenant, I got to go."

I looked at the ground and say," I just finish talking to that officer just a few minutes ago. It must be a mistake." I ask Sergeant Price if I can ride with him to the scene.

The sergeant says, "Get in Lieutenant. We got to go now."

I jumped into his vehicle and we drove off.

We arrived on the scene and it is crazy. I see two officers holding Officer Brooks' wife as she is crying and calling her husband's first name repeatedly. Officer Brooks' children are in their vehicle crying and calling for their father to get up. Two other officers are inside the carry-out holding another officer who was also crying. On the floor was Officer Brooks. The police officers had not had time to cover his body. The ambulance crew had just arrived on scene and were attempting to get to officer Brooks. I could tell in just those few seconds that a fellow officer had shot and possibly killed another brother police officer. They both worked in the same police building. How could this happen?

The investigation revealed that that Officer Brooks' wife, who was pregnant, wanted a steak and cheese sandwich from her favorite store. As officer Brooks entered the store he observed two suspects robbing the store at gun point. Officer

Brooks pointed his weapon at the two suspects and ordered them to drop their weapons and fall to the floor. The suspects followed Officer Brook's directions and fell to the floor. The store owner had activated the silent alarm. The police officers arrived on the scene and saw Officer Brook inside the store with a gun in his hand. The officers stated that they didn't see the suspects lying on the floor.

The officers entered the store with their weapons drawn and directed Officer Brooks to drop his weapon. Officer Brooks was facing away from the officers that had entered the store. Instead of Officer Brooks following the officer's directions, Officer Brooks turns towards the officers with his gun in his hand. The officers shot Officer Brooks twice in the chest killing him instantly. Officer Brooks' family observed the entire incident.

Police officers are trained to follow other police officer's directions when in such a situation. In this case, we believe that Officer Brooks felt the officers would recognize him as a police officer and they wouldn't fire upon him. That was the reason for the officer's failure to follow his training when in such a dangerous circumstance.

It was one of the lowest points in my life having to deal with such a sad incident; a family observing their loved one killed by another.

It was a very sad funeral. Officer Brooks' children all went to college and graduated. His wife never remarried. His daughter joined the police department and is doing very well. She is a detective in the Homicide Unit. Officer Brooks has 9 grandchildren.

The two officers that shot and killed Officer Brooks both retired from the department because of the incident. One of the officers had a very hard time dealing with life after retirement. He became an alcoholic. The other officer became a pastor in a church.

I still have Officer Brook's note book

Officer Helen Banks
1993
Chapter 41

Officer Helen Banks was 25 years old and very attractive. She worked for me and she always had problems and issues; not being able to work with other police officers, especially female officers, and mostly men problems. I was her Lieutenant and Sergeant Joe Williams was her immediately supervisor.

Sergeant Williams had seven officers in his squad and Officer Banks was his problem child, as the sergeant called her. Every week there was an issue concerning Officer Banks work ethic. After several months of not being able to motivate Officer Banks, the sergeant asked if I would attend a meeting with them to motivate the officer or possibly prepare to fire the officer. Firing is always the last resort, but there are some people who aren't suited for a police career.

Officer Banks was from Mississippi and had a very strong southern accent. Sergeant Williams set the meeting up in my conference room. We had already established our game plan. We both wanted to save Officer Banks' career and motivate the officer to become a good police officer. I in no way expected to hear what I heard that day at the meeting from Officer Banks.

The sergeant and I were both sitting at the conference table when Officer Banks entered the office and had a seat at the table. Before the sergeant could say anything, Officer Banks started crying. I first said to myself, *this is going to be one of those meeting, where the police officer starts crying and everybody is against me.* But after a few seconds, I could tell they were real tears and not acting.

I let the sergeant do the talking. I was going to observe and support the sergeant. I wanted the officer to know that the sergeant was in charge and not me. It was better for the situation as the officer worked for the sergeant and not directly for me.

The sergeant attempted to console Officer Banks. She held her head up and looked at me. It appeared to be genuine; when that make-up starts to run, it normally is real.

Officer Banks said, "Lieutenant, I am so sorry. I just don't know what do."

Sergeant Williams ask the officer to explain the problem. Officer Banks first said that she was a single mother living with her mother raising her 5-year-old son and things were hard.

"The child's father isn't paying no child support and my mother is unable to work." Officer Banks had assumed all the financial responsibilities in the house and her car was about to be repossessed.

Right then I said to myself, *same stuff different person.*

Then the officer looked down at the table and stopped crying. Her next comment caught me by surprise.

"Lieutenant, I am in love with Officer Michael Taylor and we just broke up. I thought we were going to get married this winter at least that is what he told me."

As Officer Banks is talking I am saying to myself, *Officer Taylor, that sorry piece of trash. That officer has dated every female officer on the Eastern Cost of America. He must have 20 children and not paying for one of them. I am surprise that he has a pay check every two weeks.*

Being his Commanding Officer, whatever is taken from his wages is sent to the police district. I am the one that will receive the same and issue the item to the officer. Officer Taylor had a different one every week it seemed. Officer Taylor was no person to cry for.

The sergeant and I continued to talk with Officer Banks to console her with her problems. I asked if she needed time off the job and offered the services of the departmental agencies that deal with those types of problems. Officer Banks stated that she was grateful and wanted to take a week off from work to think about her life.

We talk for another hour and after the conversation the sergeant and I felt good about Officer Banks comments. She further stated that she was going to get her life in order and would become a better police officer.

Officer Banks asked if we were going to the dance that the police district was sponsoring about raising money for children at Children's Hospital. The dance was that night. I told the officer that I had donated and I had other plans that night. Officer Banks smiled and thanked the sergeant and me for listing to her and understanding her problems.

After Officer Banks left the office I ask the sergeant to monitor the officer and give me an update in two weeks. I was always concerned for the welfare of my officers, sometimes too much.

If you get too involved with people's problems, you are unable to help them. I was off the next two days and was looking forward to some rest. I had a hard week and needed some break time.

The next day at approximately 8: 00 a.m. Sergeant Williams called me at home.

He said, "Lieutenant I have some bad news for you. Officer Banks committed suicide last night."

I couldn't believe it. I was just talking with this young officer no more than 20 hours ago and she sounded as if everything was going to be okay. I jumped out of the bed and the sergeant began to tell me the story.

Officer Banks had attended the dance the police district was sponsoring. On the officer's arrival she observed her ex-boyfriend, Officer Taylor, with another police female. They had dressed alike and were wearing the same jean suits. The witnesses informed the sergeant that Officer Banks became upset and confronted them. It resulted in an argument and all three police officers were directed by the supervisors that were present to leave the event and cool off.

The officers were further directed them to report to Sergeant Williams at the police district the next day. The sergeant would continue the discussion concerning their conduct. The officers were also directed to stay away from each other until then.

Officer Banks went home, took a shower, put on make-up, lied down on the bed, and shot herself in the stomach with her service weapon. This is not uncommon when women commit suicides. They still would like to be pretty when found. Very few women shoot themselves anywhere else. Men normally shoot themselves in the head when committing suicide. It was later I learned that Officer Banks was pregnant with Officer Taylor's child. Officer Banks also left a letter out-lining her reason for committing suicide. The letter simply stated that she couldn't live any longer with the rejection of Officer Taylor, knowing that she was carrying his child.

The police department is very good when an officer dies in the line of duty. They take care of the deceased officer's family very well. They pay off all the bills, the children are sent to any college in the world, the widow receives the officer's retirement, and the department stays with the family during the whole process and after. It always made me feel good, knowing that a police officer's family was okay. Sorrowfully, I have seen a lot of them.

But, when an officer commits suicide, it is like having a virus. The department will just throw you away and forget about the family. Officer's whisper your name in corners like you never where even there. Even my superiors directed that I handle it. They wanted no part of it. This made me very mad. The department wasn't even going to give Officer Banks a uniform to be buried in. Then my superiors directed that I tell the family that there was no money except the insurance that the officer carried with the government.

Officer Banks was my officer and she worked for me. We were going to do the right thing. Sergeant Williams and I visited the family the same day of the officer's death. Officer Bank's mother first told me that the Chief's assistant had visited her and told them that the police department was sorry for her daughter's death, but it was nothing they could do.

The sergeant and I made sure that Officer Banks had a uniform to be buried in. Over 500 police officers attended the funeral, including Officer Taylor. He even cried. I arranged to have Officer Banks buried without expense to the Banks family. Over 100 police cruisers escorted the Banks family to the cemetery. It was just as if the officer had died in the line of duty. I knew that some people might say that it takes away from those officers that have died in the line of duty, but as police officers, you take care of your own. This was a terrible thing to happen to a family. A young woman had taken her own life and a child had lost his mother.

The Chief of Police was there and observed everything. He just looks at me and winked. It made me feel good. The Chief of Police couldn't acknowledge my actions, but I knew where his heart was. By being the Chief of Police, he couldn't break tradition. I knew that. It was bigger than both of us. It involved 5000 police officers and years of police belief. When the Chief approached Officer Banks mother, I thought she was going to give the chief a hard time, but she didn't Ms. Banks was glad that he was there. It made her feel good. The Mayor and other dignitaries attended the funeral. This was strange, but it was an election year. The word was getting around that a lot of police officers were upset because of the disrespect that the department and city had showed Officer Banks mother.

After the funeral Officer Taylor was given a hard time by many officers in the police district. They felt that Officer Taylor showed bad taste in his actions. But time has a way of resolving all problems, I guess.

I used to think about Officer Banks often the next few years. I wanted to believe that I did everything that I could to help the officer. In my mind I felt that I had, but there was always that uncertainty.

Several years later, after I had retired from the police department I oversaw school security at a local High school. This young man walked into my office and wanted a parking pass for his vehicle to park on the school grounds. When the young man gave me his school identification, it read Melvin Banks, the same name as Officer Helen Banks' son. I asked the young man if anybody in his family was on the Metropolitan Police Department in Washington, DC. Melvin stated that his mother was a police officer and she had died. His mother had accidently shot and killed herself while cleaning her weapon.

I told Melvin that I knew his mother and she was a very good police officer and we use to work together years ago while in Washington, DC. Melvin and I talk for approximately two hours in my office about his mother, because he was a little boy when she died and he had forgotten so much about her.

The next two years Melvin and I become very good friends while he attended High School. Sergeant Williams and I really enjoyed watching him graduated from High School. His mother would have been so proud of her son. Melvin's father also came back into his life after his mother's death. He sent his son to college where Melvin became a teacher. Melvin's grandmothers thanked Sergeant William's and me for not telling Melvin the truth about the event.

This was one of those times that it felt good to go back in my early years as a policeman and see something as beautiful as a child growing up and becoming a good man. It stills touches me even today.

The Big Chase
1994
Chapter 42

I was the Watch Commander, Seventh District; a person that oversees the police district. It was approximately 8:30 p.m. I was feeling good and everything was going ok; no shootings, assaults, and serious crimes reported. It was a good night. I spoke to soon.

Sergeant James Crook, in a very loud and scared voice, reported to the dispatcher that he was chasing a blue truck and the driver, Mr. John Denver, was wanted for attempted murder. They were driving southbound on South Capitol Street heading towards Maryland. The chase was on.

By this time several other police units had joined in the chase. Not only the units assigned to the Seventh District but units that were in the immediately area not assigned to the district. We even had other police departments join in the chase, such as the United States Park Police, who patrol the adjoining area.

When Sergeant Crook and the vehicle that he was chasing reached the Maryland line, we had approximately 10 police vehicles involved in the chase. The sergeant then advised the dispatcher that Mr. Crook was shooting a firearm as he was driving the vehicle.

On reaching the Maryland line, the Maryland police joined in the chase. Mr. Denver fired at the Maryland Police Officers. When I reached the location, all I could see were police vehicles, with their sirens blasting and red lights flashing. I said to myself that this was getting totally out of hand and I didn't want anyone to get hurt.

As if things couldn't get any worse, the Chief of Police and the Assistant Chief of Police came over the air and advised the dispatcher that they were joining in the chase. I had forgotten that the chiefs were in the district attending a meeting with a community group.

Now the chase is in Maryland, another jurisdiction, and I not only have my police units involved but several different police agencies and the two top police officials on the Metropolitan Police Department as well along with shots being fired by the suspect. This is not a normal police chase.

A few minutes go by and the chase goes over the Wilson Bridge, which links Maryland, Washington, and Virginia, in the direction of Virginia, another state. Things couldn't get any worse.

The chase moves into Virginia and Virginia State Troopers join in the chase. We now have approximately 20 police vehicles involved in the chase, with the Chief of Police as the last vehicle in the chase attempting to keep up. Police officers were yelling over the radio and everyone attempting to talk at the same time. Mr. Denver fired several more shots at the police.

Mr. Denver reached and turned onto Eisenhower Avenue, almost turning the vehicle over. All 20 police vehicles are in close pursuit. He drove into a residential neighborhood. Luckily no one is on the streets or walking in the area.

Mr. Denver stops in front of a house and turns the vehicle around facing the police officers. They had blocked the street off and there were no other exits. Mr. Denver stopped for a moment and guns the engine without his vehicle moving.

All the police officers exited their vehicles and formed a semi half-moon shape, facing Mr. Denver's vehicle. Before I can reach the location, Mr. Denver drives his vehicle toward the police officers at a very high rate of speed. The police officers all fire their weapons, striking Mr. Denver's vehicle.

I had signaled and directed the sergeant that was following me to block off the street to ensure that no one left the scene before I could talk with them.

Mr. Denver then drove his vehicle into a nearby house to escape the gun fire, causing a large amount of damage to the structure. The officers rushed the vehicle and amazingly Mr. Denver isn't harmed. Later investigation revealed that the officers fired approximately 60 rounds into the vehicle.

By this time, the Chief of Police had arrived on scene and he wasn't happy. He told me that he would be waiting for this investigation to be completed. He saw the whole thing and he didn't want any bull crap from me about what happen. All I could say was, "Yes Sir" and that I would get the police officers back into the District of Columbia as soon as the scene is processed. The Chief said, "Ok" and just started looking at everybody as they were attempting to process the scene. He stayed in one spot for approximately one hour, just looking with the assistant chief stood next him.

This didn't bother me very much. I just made sure everything went by the numbers. I knew the chief and he was a good man and fair, but if things went wrong, he held you accountable for your actions.

The chief didn't like the idea of his officers being in another jurisdiction and involved in a police shooting.

As I was talked to Mr. Thomas, the owner of the house that Mr. Denver had struck, he informed me that this was the third time in three years that the police had chased someone and the suspects had driven into his home and in the same spot. He laughed and said, "I guess it was God's will." Mr. Thomas was a pastor and took the incident very well.

I said to myself, "Hell with that. Who would be paying for my house?"

Mr. Denver only received minor injuries when he backed into Mr. Thomas's home and back pain, but no gunshot wounds. After 60 shots and no injury, he was a very lucky man. His vehicle was searched and we located a sawed-off shotgun that we learned later had been used in the shooting of a store clerk that he had robbed and killed the night before.

Sergeant Crook closed another good case. He was always involved in car chases, at least once a week. The sergeant caught most of them. The sergeant could look at a car and tell you if the car was stolen or wanted in a crime.

Mr. Denver pled guilty to murder and armed robbery. We connected him to another 20 armed robbery cases. Mr. Thomas' home was repaired at the expense to the Metropolitan Police Department and Sergeant Crook retired several years later without a scratch on him. He served approximately 35 years on the force. The Chief of Police also retired a few years after the incident. I still see the chief even today at police events, funerals, and retirements. The chief always brings this case up. One day I am going to tell him to give it a break, maybe. He still retired as a Chief of Police, to you retired police officer you know what I mean.

Can You Help A Friend?
1993
Chapter 43

"You are my friend as a friend will always be my friend"
LT Marco F. Kittrell, MPDC, (ret)

I was sitting in my office drinking coffee and reviewing police incident reports. It was approximately 6:30 p.m. on a Friday evening. It was a great day and everything was going well. We had not had any shootings or serious incidents that required me to leave the office. I was fully staffed with police officers and I had three sergeants working on the street. I even had time to watch the evening news. What more could I ask for? It was a good time to be a Lieutenant. I had no idea how this day would test my values.

The desk sergeant called me and said that one of the retired officers wanted to come and see me. The desk sergeant is the person that supervises the police station and the administrative processes. All visitors must go through their office before entering any other part of the building.

I didn't even ask who it was. I said, "Sure send him up to my office."

I always liked talking to retired officers. They always made me feel good. Most of the retired officers were from the same school and value system that I came from and we talked the same talked.

I looked up from my desk and Detective James White enters the office. I was glad to see him. I hadn't seen or talked to the detective in about three years. He was one of my role models. He taught me a lot about police work and how you conduct yourself as a police officer. Detective White probably was one of the best detectives that the police department ever had.

Detective White walked in and said, "Lieutenant Kittrell it is really good to see you, I haven't seen you for about three years."

We began talking and talked about an hour. We talked about the old days on the department, me as a young officer, and all the things that he had experienced as a police officer; just two old guys chewing the fat, as they use to say. I still considered myself young, but after 22 years in the department, I felt like one of the senior officers that had been around the block a few times.

I didn't want to talk about children. I knew that the detective had some bad luck with his two children. His son, while driving to college, was hit by a drunk driver and killed on impact. His family just had Christmas vacation together and his son wanted to get back to school. His son has been dead for four years.

The detective and his wife took it very hard. Their son was the oldest and the first child in his family to attend college. I remembered the cook-out that his family had given the young man before he drove off to college. His father was very proud of his children, especially his son.

Now his daughter, Mary was another story. I knew that she had taken the wrong path in life. Mary started using drugs at an early stage in her life. She paid for them by stealing, then selling drugs, and finally prostitution. After the detective retired from the department, he and his wife relocated to North Carolina, their original home. Mary stayed in the area and went to college. At first everything was ok. Mary was doing well and there was no evidence that she would get in trouble.

She came from a good family, was head strong and was always doing the right thing. Mary met the wrong young man in college and it went all downhill from there. Mary's parents did everything that a loving family could do, but it was too late, once she got hooked on drugs and crack. She never came back to them. It was a shame because Mary was always on the fast track and her family expected great things from her.

As we were talking, Detective White asked how my children were doing. I said just fine, they were all doing great things, and I was proud of them. During the conversation about my children he kept looking at the floor. I didn't want to dwell on the subject too long because of his children.

I ask him, "Do you want to take a ride and get something to eat?"

He said, "No, but can you do me a favor?"

I said, "Sure. What is it?"

"Marco, you know my daughter has been selling herself on the block for the last year and I just want to go and get my baby and take her home. My wife is sick and the doctors said that she would be dead in about six months. I just would like for my wife to see our daughter home and get herself together."

I told him, "That's great that you are still attempting to work with Mary and help her. There is nothing like a parent's love."

Before I could finish talking, he stopped me and said, "Marco, I am going to go and get my daughter, take her by force if need be, throw her in the back of my car, and take her home. Whatever it takes, I am not going to lose my last child. I owe this to my family. I can't sleep, eat, or even look at myself in the mirror anymore. It is just killing me that my child is living this way. My wife is sick and dying I have nothing else to live for."

"White," I said, "I know that you are hurting inside and I would love to help you anyway I can, legally, but your daughter is 22 years old, a grown woman, an adult, and she can go and live anywhere she would like. You can't ask the Seventh District Watch Commander to go with you, while in uniform, in a police car, and kidnap your grown daughter. There are laws against such things, daughter or not. I have one daughter and I don't know what I would do if my child was in the same situation. Probably the same thing you are thinking. I hope a friend would tell me the same thing that I am telling you. Man, don't do it.

"Those streets have gotten her now and you know once those streets grab you, it will take those streets to let her go, when she is ready. Yes, talk to her, pray to God every day, and if we are lucky, she will come home. But, not this way, White. We both will go to jail and I am not going to let anyone that I care about do something stupid. Let's talk about this some more. Man, you have too much to lose.

Detective White answered, "I have already lost everything; my son, my wife and my daughter. What else do I have?"

"I said, "Your daughter is still here. Problems yes, but she is still alive and so is your wife. You have good memories, a great career, and yourself. You are a young man. Many people look up to you, including me."

Detective White started crying. I grabbed him. I suggest that he go and talk with his daughter and I will stand by looking over his shoulder. He stops crying and thanks me for the kind words. He just couldn't bear to lose his last family member.

Detective White collected himself, went to the men's room, returned to my office, and said, "Lieutenant, I am ready. Let's go and talk to my daughter. I am so glad that I made you my friend. It just might pay off. We both laughed."

We get into the police cruiser and I could see that the detective started getting very nervous. I wondered if I was doing the right thing. All I could think about was my daughter and I thanked God for not being in this situation.

We reached the corner that Mary was working. I knew it well. I used to check on her daily, when I had the chance. It would hurt me knowing that my friend's child was living the life that she was. It was a very terrible thing to see. Mary had been arrested several times. I had even seen her with her customers. It took everything out of me that I could not to do something, but I was a police officer, professional not personal.

We saw Mary. She didn't even recognize her father as he walked up to her. Mary looked like something the dog bought into the house. She was a cheap thrill, but all I could see was that 10-year-old little girl running to her father as he finished work and his wife picked him up at the police district. Mary would run out of the car to her father, yelling daddy. He would pick her up, kiss his child, and get into the car with his wife driving away. I used to say, *what a lucky man.*

Detective White talked to his daughter for one hour. She walked away, saying, 'Daddy go home and leave me alone."

The detective is just destroyed. He gets back into the police car and said, "Marco, I am ready to go home. It is in God's hand."

I drive my friend back to his car. He thanked me and he said that he was going back home to care for his wife. We said nothing else concerning his daughter.

Detective White's wife died seven months later. Mary was killed during an argument over money with another prostitute, one month after her mother died. Detective White came for his daughter and buried her in North Carolina next to his wife and son.

Every day after that incident, and even before, it made me very protective of my children, especially my daughter. I love all my children, but I always kept an extra eye on my daughter, right or wrong. That's just the way it was. I said a prayer for Detective White. I wish I knew where he was, just to say hi.

They Are All Gone
Chapter 44

"Let me go by the way of my friends for I am with them"
LT Marco F. Kittrell, MPDC, (ret)

I was sitting in my office when Sergeant Michael Waters called. He invited me to breakfast and I accepted. He stated that he would meet me at the Greater Southeast Hospital located on Southern Avenue in South East. This was the only really decent place to eat at the time in the area. The sergeant had retired in 1990 and we always kept in contact. I arrived before the sergeant and started ordering my food, as always. He arrived as the pancakes were almost ready. It always happened this way. Whenever we had breakfast the sergeant would enter the restaurant at the same time as the pancakes were about finish. I always ordered a stack for him. This was our routine for 10 years. He was a good friend and one of the old boys. Old school all the way and I loved to talk and share stories with him.

As we are sitting at the table, I noticed that the sergeant wasn't looking that well. I didn't say anything. By this time, I had gotten used to seeing some of the retired officers looking shocking. I always said it was caused by drinking too much, too many women, running the streets, not eating the proper foods, stress, paying child support, and everything else that you could think of.

Sergeant Waters did all the above and then some, but he was a good man and had a good heart. The sergeant had three children by three different women and took care of them all. They loved him and he had special relationships with all his children, but the sergeant never married.

As we are talking, and for no apparent reason, the sergeant started talking about the old crew; officers that we had worked with over the years. His voice changed, became very serious, and looked as if he was carrying some secret and wanted to get it off his chest. I could have asked him, but I knew the sergeant. He was a very proud man and somewhat secretive concerning himself, especially if it was bad news. I knew if we talked enough he would tell me sooner or later.

The sergeant says, "Lieutenant, do you remember Sergeant John Davis? That was a crazy guy, always getting in stuff. He must have been involved in seven police shootings that we knew about.

"How about Sergeant Kettering, that lazy fucker! I don't know how in the hell he made sergeant. He never did any real police work except investigating the local bars for possible violations relating to them closing on time. They couldn't, because he was always in the bar drinking after hours. We should have fired that boy!

"Do you remember Captain Jenkins? We use to call him the bible thumper; always talking about God, church, and family. He was a good captain when it came to police work, except when he was chasing police women. I don't believe any women got past the captain.

"Then there was Officer Wayne, that officer was from West Virginia. He couldn't figure out what he wanted to do, police work or preacher. I have seen that officer kick the crap out of someone and then preach to them when he got the person at the police district. I even saw that boy pray with a few prisoners. Hell of a thing to see.

"My favorite officer was John Day. That fucker would party all night, come to work, arrest everything that moved, go to court, and after leaving the court sleep for two hours. That was all he needed, two hours. I just couldn't understand him. The things that he did will go down in history."

The sergeant goes on for about thirty minutes, calling off names of policemen that we had worked with or had knowledge of their episodes as police officers. Then it hit me, every officer that he has talked about has died. The whole conversation isn't like our normal conversation.

At some point the sergeant stopped talking, looked at me, and said, "Kittrell, I got the cancer. The doctor gave me two months. It has spread too fast. It is just my time to go and see my maker. I wish I had another few years. I would love to see my children married and have children. It just wasn't enough time. You don't think about such things until it is your time to check out."

Before I could respond, the sergeant said, "Also, I want you to have something; my retirement badge, the one that the police department gave me. I have great kids, but I know you will take care of it."

I was unable to say anything. My friend just told me that he was dying and would be gone in a few months. The sergeant goes on to tell me, "Don't worry about me. I am 60 years old and had a great life. Think of all the women that I have known. Do you remember Jennie, that wild cat I used to date back in 1974? Now that was a real woman, crazy as hell, would cut you, but at night, made me feel like a man. I am just so sorry that she married that fireman. I never really trusted that women."

We started laughing. We finish our meal and the sergeant stated that he had something to do and he would call me tomorrow.

The next day never came. I would call my friend and he never returned my phone calls. One month later I learned that the sergeant had been admitted to the hospital. I immediately visited my friend and the doctors stated that the sergeant didn't have much time. He probably wouldn't make through the night.

I stayed with him for three hours and only left when the staff told me to go; only family could stay.

Before leaving the sergeant, he asked if I had seen any of the old guys lately.

I said, "Yes Sir, and they always ask about Sergeant Walters." The sergeant smiled and grabbed my hand. My friend died that night with his children by his side and their mothers. I never received the sergeant's retirement badge, but that I was okay. I had my memories.

My Retirement Dinner

The Red Sports Car 1995

Chapter 45

It was my retirement party and I was very happy. My wife had worked very hard on it and many our friends and family were there. My brother, Baron and his wife, Brenda had allowed us to use their home and this made me feel very good, knowing that my mother, children, brothers, and sister were involved in my retirement party as well.

As I was giving my speech, thanking everyone for their support over the past 24 years as a policeman, I started to look around room. Every face that I saw had a story, but when I saw Sergeant Mike Joseph, I thought about his red sports car.

It was 1975 and I was a rookie. I had just graduated from the police academy only two weeks earlier and assigned to the First District. One of the district's responsibilities was Capitol Hill. I knew the area well. I had patrolled the area as a police cadet in the early seventies.

The United States Capitol had been bombed twice during that time and I was on the scene of both bombings; once in 1972 and again in 1974. In 1972, a terrorist group known as the Red Patron left a small bomb in the men's bathroom, causing minor damage but no injuries. In 1974, they bombed the bathroom again, causing the same affects; I guess they didn't like bathrooms.

The area was also known for where many congressman and their staff members lived. That is another story. I was accustomed to dealing with congressmen, senators, and their staff members. They were just like any other people, needing a little attention now and then.

Officer Mike Joseph was assigned as one of my training officers. Officer Joseph was a good officer, but he had problems at home. His wife was cheating on him and sometimes when he came to work you could tell by his facial express that it wasn't going to be a good day.

I was a rookie and as such when you were assigned to a senior officer they ran the show, no questions asked. Most of the senior officers were hard on the new officers, but they all meant well, including Officer Joseph.

When Officer Joseph and I worked together he never spoke about his personal problems. I was a rookie and what advise could I offer him? He had been a police officer for seven years and he acted the part. That's just how it was back in those days. Time in grade meant a great deal and officers treated you according to your time in grade.

Having been a police cadet for three years I knew the rules, so this initiation process didn't bother me that much. I knew that the police officers wanted you to be successful in your rookie year.

I knew that Officer Joseph was having problems at home. When he and the other senior officers would meet while working, the officers would drive to a location, exit their cars and walk away and start their conversation about each other problems, but never in front of the rookies. We were told to stay in the vehicles and listen to the radio, but if dispatch called, never answer the radio. You had to call the senior officer and they would talk on the radio, but never the rookie.

During their secret conversations, I could always hear their conversation. I tell you, those officers had some serious problems. Wife's cheating on them, girlfriends pregnant, bills stacking up, children on drugs, no money, house about to be foreclosed, and the sergeant on their ass and on and on. I said to myself, *these guys got some serious issues*.

I will say this, they all attempted to help each other and I respected them for that. But Officer Joseph always scared me. When he talked about his wife, his voice was always the most serious. The officers would laugh at each other's problem together but, never at each other. Officer Joseph never laughed.

A month later we were working the midnight tour of duty, 12am to 8am, the graveyard shift. It took me a whole year to get use to the shift. I used to say, it wasn't normal for people to be up past 2 a.m., working.

On this particular night, Officer Joseph and I are working together. Once you relieved the officers that were working the earlier shift, you always advised the dispatcher that you were ready for service. On this night, Officer Joseph didn't do that. He just started driving. As a rookie, I didn't say anything.

Officer Joseph drove to his house, which is out of the district and across the city. He didn't say anything to me either. Once we reached his home, he exited the police vehicle and started starring at his red sports car that is parked in the driveway. He watched his car for approximately one hour and then he placed his right hand over his firearm. That's when I got scared.

I knew of police officers that had done some dumb things over the year. I told myself that I wasn't going to be part of any act of stupidly by a police officer. I exited the police vehicle very slowly, because I didn't want to spook Officer Joseph. I felt that it was a very difficult time in his life. I walk over to him and sat on the vehicle next to him. The officer started smoking a cigarette and looked at me.

"Officer Kittrell, are your married? Do you have any kids?"

"I'm married and got two boys.

"That is good. Are you happy with your family? My family life has gone to shit. My wife, Kim, will not have any babies. To top it all off, the bitch is fucking some other motherfucker and she is driving my red sports car to meet her man. Now that is a mother for you, isn't it?"

I don't get a chance to respond because the officer continued to talk.

"Kittrell, that bitch isn't going to drive my car tonight and doing her thing. I tried to have sex with her before work and she said that she wasn't feeling good. Said she was going to a girlfriend's house to listen to some music, just she and some of her girlfriends.

"I just looked at the bitch. I love her and I try to believe what that lying women is telling me, but I realize that it is a lie and she has a boyfriend. I found the guy's wallet in my sports car. My wife forgets that I am a policeman."

He smiled as he is looking at me.

"That was when I started following her to the guy's apartment. Every Monday and Friday and today is Friday. She normally stays for two hours.

That was when I got scared. I said, *God give me the wisdom and strengths to do the right thing.*

"Kittrell, you want to hear some more shit? My fucking wife brought me the damn car and now she is driving my red sports car to meet and fuck her boyfriend."

The officer had a look that I would see again and again

in my police career. We called it the "1000-mile look." That's when a police officer looks right through you and just don't care. I knew I had to do something, but didn't know what it was.

I said, "Mike, I can't begin to imagine what you are going through and I don't know what I would do in your situation, but I wouldn't let my wife get the best of me. I would just leave and start over with someone new."

I don't know if that was the best thing to say, but it was all that I had and I went for it. I had nothing else to offer. I was concentrating on not letting this officer get us both arrested because of his cheating wife. I had a family and I had planned to retire 20 years later.

Officer Joseph bites his teeth, throws the cigarette to the ground, and keeps his right hand on his service weapon. A few seconds go by and to my relief the officer said, "Let's get the fuck out of here. That's it! I will be leaving that cheating bitch in the morning."

We get back in the police cruiser and drove back to our district. The remainder of the tour we didn't speak another word about the event. We were very busy as most Friday's are, but not one word about his wife. Prior to check off, I had to tell someone.

I informed one of the senior officers about the incident and he thanked me. He and several other senior officers asked Joseph to accompany them to breakfast. He agreed. Officer

Joseph and the other officers drove by my car as I about to leave the parking lot. They asked if I was hungry and said they were paying. I smiled and immediately said, "Ok, let's go." It made me feel like one of the boys in that they had invited me to dine with them.

We stayed in the restaurant for three hours and I enjoyed myself. During the breakfast, Officer Joseph stated that he was going to leave his wife that day, which he did. Prior to leaving, Officer Joseph shook my hand and said, "Thanks Marco."

We never talked about the incident for the next twenty years. During our careers, we always stayed in contact. Officer Joseph remarried, had three children, and 10 grandchildren.

During my retirement celebration, Sergeant Joseph, who had retired in 1990 and relocated to North Carolina, took me to the side and said, "Lieutenant, back in 1975, you never knew what you did for me. You probably save my career and life. I was angry and ready to kill that woman, but God had other plans. You were there. I have enjoyed my life and always thought of you. I just wanted to say, 'thanks.'" His remarks caught me totally off-guard and I will never forget his kind words.

He told me that Kim had died of cancer five years earlier and he attended her funeral. I believe that Sergeant Joseph still loved her. When he talked about Kim, his eyes got very weak and red. It was not for me to judge. It was many years ago and we all have gone on with our lives.

I thanked God for being there for the both of us. The sergeant thanked me but I thank God for giving us both the courage to make the right decision that day, especially Sergeant Joseph. He was a good man, but he was in love. I respected that.

Sergeant Walter Johnson
1975
Chapter 46

Sergeant Johnson was my sergeant for two years and he motivated me in becoming the man that I am today. He never knew what he instilled in me or the drive that only materializes when a person is confronted with such a dramatic experience in one's life.

I was 20 years old and just graduated from the police academy. I was assigned to the First District, located in the Capitol Hill area of Washington, DC. I was full of confidence and vigor. I had been a police cadet for three years and was very excited about the opportunity of serving the community and making my family proud of me.

My first day on the job, I was scheduled to report for duty at 6 a.m. I was there at 4 a.m. I was so excited and looking forward to being a police officer. I really wanted to do well.

When I first walked into the roll call room, I was received as all new rookies were received, with revulsion. I knew what to expect. I knew the ritual of a rookie as a police officer. When I entered the room, one officer said, "I will be got-damn, the police department has resorted to hiring young boys from the reform school. I know this mother-fucker don't even have a damn permit to drive. What is your name boy?"

I just smiled and said, "Officer Marco Kittrell, sir."

"That is one stupid name for a boy. Was you on drugs?"

All the officers started laughing. One officer remarked that, "at least the bitch has manners."

I was told to take the seat in the far rear of the room, "don't say shit," and just look like I know what is going on. I complied with my orders and took my seat. I knew the rules of the game.

Sergeant Johnson entered the roll call room and all the talking stopped. That was my first meeting with the sergeant. He gave all the officers their assignments and told me that I will be with Officer James Hawkins for the week, who will be my training officer.

After roll call the sergeant told me to follow him to his office. Once there, the sergeant asked me several questions, explained what he expected from me, and told me if I have any problems to feel free to come to him and we would be able to work through any problem. The conversation made me feel good about him and myself.

Sergeant Walter Johnson 1975

The next twelve months was my foundation for the police force. Whenever I was involved in something, Sergeant Johnson was there giving me instructions. It felt good that I had someone who took a great deal of concern in my career.

One case I received was an assignment for a lost child. On my arrival, I was told by the parents that their 5-year-old little girl was missing. The parents fell asleep and when they awoke, the rear door was open and the little girl was missing.

I and other officers searched the entire neighborhood and we couldn't find the child. Approximately 50 people in the area assisted in the search. By the time Sergeant Johnson arrived on the scene the media had arrived. It started to get dark and everyone started thinking the worst.

On being advised of the situation, Sergeant Johnson asked if I had looked under the child's bed. My partner and I felt this didn't make any sense. We assumed that the parents had searched the child's bedroom.

Over 200 people had gathered in front of the parent's home; even the family pastor. He started praying in front of the house. My sergeant wanted us to search the child's bedroom. I said to myself, *the sergeant lost it this time.*

The sergeant walked up the steps smoking his cigarette and drinking his coffee. He walked into the child's bedroom and looked under the child's bed. To everyone's surprise the child was asleep on the floor. The sergeant called to me and my partner and told us to come to the bedroom.

The sergeant looked at me and my partner and told us, "Don't worry, this is not the first-time police officers failed to look at the obvious. Also, many children that are reported lost are hiding somewhere in the house at the time that they are reported lost. So even if the parents reported that they had searched the house, the officers have to search it as well."

My partner and I did search the child's room but never under the bed. We were looking for signs of foul play, not a child hiding.

Sergeant Johnson walked outside and told the crowd that the child had been located and she is okay. Everyone started clapping and praising God for the child's recovery. We never told the crowd that the child had been sleeping the entire time. Sergeant Johnson gave a great speech praising the officers for their hard work and dedication to their job. The pastor asked that everyone go home and gave thanks for the child's recovery.

Sergeant Johnson walked to his car like a general, looked back at me, smiled, and drove away. He never said anything negative to me about that day or to anyone else. He would just smile every now and then when he saw me for the next 20 years.

I always remembered that day. The sergeant taught me a great deal about being a police officer and a professional. He came to my retirement party 20 years later and I just knew that he was going to tell everyone about that case, but he didn't. He just gave me a lot of praise.

That was the kind of man he was. When I was promoted to sergeant and lieutenant, he always called me by my rank, never my first name. It was an honor to be associated with Sergeant Johnson.

The Full Moon 1977

Chapter 47

While at my retirement party, Sergeant Terrance Tompkins and I began talking about when we first graduated from the police academy and we started working in the field. The sergeant was one of my good friends and reminded me of our days as young police officers.

The sergeant asked if I remembered the full moon nights. How could I forget? We use to say mad people were out tonight. People acted so differently when the moon was full. Fights, stabbings, shootings; everything you could think of happened on those nights.

The worst fights that I was ever involved in occurred on those nights. I remembered one night, Terrance and I were working and we received a radio assignment for a husband and wife fighting at 2310 Hoard Road Southeast.

On our arrival, we were met by a Ms. Jane Bird. She asked us to come in and started pointing at her husband. Mr.

Bird was asleep with his head lying on the table in the dining room. I asked Ms. Bird, "What's the issue with your husband?"

She said, "You can't see, he is drunk? Lock his ass up."

Now Terrance and I know you can't arrest a person for being intoxicated in their own home. We attempted to explain this to Ms. Bird, but she wasn't satisfied with our response.

Consequently, she told us to get the hell out of her house since we weren't going to do anything about her husband. As we were walking out the door, and for no apparent reason, Ms. Bird threw hot fish grease on us. We should have noticed the grease on the stove; a good police officer is always aware of their surroundings.

Subsequently, as we are arresting Ms. Bird, all hell broke loose. Mr. Bird woke up yelling, "Get off my wife" and started fighting Terrence and me. During the struggle, the Birds, Terrence, and I fell down the steps and into the street.

Several young men observed the struggle and yelled, "Those fucking police are beating up the Birds!"

Then several other people in the area attempted to stop us from making the arrest. I had to call for back-up. Once the other police officers arrived, we arrested 15 people. Now this wasn't a normal full-moon night, but close to it.

In contrast to full moon nights, whenever the Washington Redskins football team played, everything went dead. Radio assignments, crimes, and the need for police services were reduced by 60 about percent. As soon as the game was over, calls resumed. Shootings, stabbings, assaults, and crime resumed. It was the strangest thing you ever saw.

Tex

1982

Chapter 48

When I first came on the department in 1972, I used to love to listen to the World War II veteran police officers talk. At the time, the World War II officers were not young men; they were from 50 to 60. World War II occurred 27 years earlier and these officers were in their teens when they join the military. They were funny guys.

There was this one World War II veteran that we called Tex. He wasn't from Texas. He was Washington, DC, born, raised, educated, worked, and lived. He loved Washington, DC, and he loved being a policeman. He had been on the force for approximately 22 years when I first met him in 1972.

Tex loved telling stories about the war, police incidents, and him. The one thing that I admired about Tex was that he wasn't afraid to laugh at himself.

He always said, "Nothing is wrong with the truth, except a lie. That would be the problem."

In 1974, I asked Tex how he got the name Tex, in that he was from Washington. His answer is one of my favorite stories.

Tex said, "Ten years ago, approximately 1964, I was assigned to the White House for a guard detail. President Lyndon Johnson was about to give a speech and the department were short of police officers for the detail. Back then, the Washington Police Department provided security for not only the city, but the white House and the Capitol and other federal buildings. Now all those locations have their own police forces.

"Police officers in those days wore long police coats and we used to store our pistols in our coat pockets. This allowed us to get our weapons out faster, if we needed the weapon.

"I am standing in the rear of the room as President Johnson is giving his speech to the press. Thirty-eight Specials, then like now, have very sensitive triggers. You know it doesn't take much to pull the trigger. I had my hands in my pockets and I accidently pull the trigger.

"The secret service grabbed the President and threw him down to the ground. Everyone with a gun pulled their firearm out looking for someone to shoot. I am just standing in the corner looking up in the sky as if nothing is going on.

"Now, you may remember that the thirty-eight special generates a lot of smoke when you discharge the same. There was so much smoke it looked like a damn fire was in the room.

The secret service rushed the President out of the room and one female report shouted, 'That crazy-ass police officer attempted to shoot the president.' I knew this didn't look and sound good.

"I shouted, "No, my weapon discharged accidently' as the secret service agents rushed me. All I wanted to do was hide under a rock, but there were none to be found.

"The Secret Service investigated the incident and verified my story, but my troubles had just started. President Johnson was informed of the accident and asked to speak with me prior to him leaving the White House. The President had a good laugh over the incident and told me that he had a few miss-fires himself."

As Tex had said, that was only the beginning of his problems. He had to deal with the Metropolitan Police Department. In those days and during my tenure, one thing you didn't do was disgrace the department or yourself while working on a high-profile detail or investigation. It was just not tolerated.

Turns out it was Tex's lucky day. People from the White House called the Chief of Police and told him that they wanted to keep the incident very quiet, in that it was very embarrassing to all involved. The chief agreed and said it would not happen.

When Tex return to police headquarters, as we called the police districts in those days, the commanding officer told

Tex that he had a new assignment. Tex was assigned to walk the foot beat on Texas Avenue, Southeast. The commander further stated that regardless of snow, rain, hell freezing over, or the world coming to an end, Tex would walk that foot beat.

It was a lousy assignment. There wasn't anything there but woods and street traffic. He wasn't allowed to leave his beat under any circumstances. It got so bad, Tex had to find other means to use the bathroom. During the 1968 riots, the police force worked 24 hours and all over the city, but not Tex. He walked his Texas Avenue beat. Tex said he used to watch police cars go by on emergency runs, but he just walked the beat.

Police officers started calling him Tex after his Texas Avenue foot beat. Tex always said, "Kittrell, Don't fuck up. The police department is a mean mother."

That was one thing Tex taught me; laugh at yourself, learn from your mistakes, and teach others not only what not to do, but what to do and how to do it better. I believe in that today.

The Metropolitan Police Department made Tex walk that foot beat for 10 years, but he never complained or said anything bad about the police department. Tex believed that as a member of the Metropolitan Police Force, you should be proud to serve the department and do your best to serve proudly. Whatever happened as you traveled down that road was just the way it was.

Tex retired in 1980 and died in 1990. Miss you man and our great times. You had a great career and influenced me.

I made it.

The Wall

1982

Chapter 49

The Vietnam Veterans Memorial was dedicated on November 13, 1982. It was a glorious week with celebrations, speeches, and many people visiting the great city of Washington, DC. There were so many veterans in the city you felt like you were in an army camp.

At the time, a large amount of police offers on the force were Vietnam Veterans. They were all close and they could relate to each other's personal problems when it came to the war.

After the Wall was completed many veterans started visiting the Wall. Then veterans started committing suicide while at the Wall.

This was a very strange but sad occurrence. I can't begin to total the number of suicides that occurred. The police department stationed a police guard around the Wall in an attempt to stop the suicides.

By this time, I had responded to many suicides so they weren't strange to me, but this was so unusual. As I talked to the Vietnam veteran police officers, they all related to the suicides and they started telling me stories about the war. It wasn't a pretty picture.

It wasn't like the World War II veterans. Their stories were always uplifting; country, flag, mom, and the girl next door kind of stuff. Yes, they had some sad stories too, but not all their stories were negative.

The Vietnam veterans were sad. Everyone they talked about was either dead, on drugs, contracted an illness, or didn't come home. I am not talking bad about these guys and gals. They served their country and merited our respect and gratitude, but as a young man I just observed a difference between the two types of veterans.

As a police officer in the 1970's, many police calls involving Vietnam veterans involved some type of violence, I am sorry to say. I was a skinny young officer weighing approximately 170 ponds. These guys were trained to hurt people and they knew how to hurt you.

I remember one incident at the bus station. I walked a foot beat at the station. I didn't like my assignment, especially in the evening. Every tour there was always a problem. When the bus pulled into the parking lot, the driver would wave his hand out the window, signaling for some help from the police. I used to say, not again. I knew what to expect.

The Wall 1982

The bus didn't make it all the way into the station. He stopped right in the middle of the parking lot and yells out the window, "Officer you better come and get this crazy motherfucker off this bus."

All the passengers ran off the bus; some of them were crying. I immediately ran on to the bus and I see a young man, with no clothes on, performing some karate moves. He was built like a young Mike Tyson.

He looks at me and started yelling, "Charlie!"

I has been in several fights with the veterans and I knew what Charlie meant; the enemy.

The man ran towards me and slipped on something on the floor. I never knew what it was and didn't care. I jumped on the man and the bus driver did too. It wasn't pretty but it worked. We subdued the man just as my backup arrived. It took them only three minutes to get there, but it seemed like 3 hours. Any police officer can tell you about this.

This was only one incident and it in no way reflects negatively on the men and women that served in Vietnam. I am just pointing out that as a young police officer, when I had to address certain incidents concerning some veterans who were mentally damage or under some type of illegal drug, it was always a challenge.

The police officers that were Vietnam veterans always showed compassion when dealing with these veterans, even when they were extremely violent. I always respected them for their empathy.

I was never in the military and couldn't relate to their experiences as they could, but I will never forget their sympathy for their fellow veterans.

To all the men and women that were killed or damaged because of the Vietnam War, we as a country owe you our gratefulness and respect for serving your country. I can still see the young men that had committed suicide after visiting the Vietnam Veterans Memorial. It is something I just wanted to comment on in that I wanted to remember them.

My Children and Grandchildren
Chapter 50

My wife and I have five children and eight grandchildren. They are very important to us and have always been a strong part of our life.

During my career, I always thought of my children. I never wanted to leave them without a father. I wanted to be there for them and see our children grow and mature into the adults that I knew they could become.

I saw too many police families without fathers and it always appeared that there was a void in the children's lives. I just couldn't imagine not being there for my children. That desire sometimes dictated how I did my job. I was never negligent in my duties, but that desire to always be with my children was a strong influence in how I did my job.

On many occasions, I took chances that endangered my life, which was my job and duty to my fellow police officers. As a younger officer, I didn't understand fear until I experienced the horror of humanity. I always said that when a police officer tells me that they have never been scared, I just look at them and smile. I have been scared, but was never a coward and never deferred from my duties as a police officer.

I have been shot, stabbed, beaten, run over by a vehicle, and even chased by dogs, but I always did my job as a police officer. The desire in Man to be with their children and never abandon them by being killed in the line of duty was my driving force to survive. My fate was in God's hands and I knew he had me covered. He was my captain and I never lost faith in his guidance. If I listened, I would be there for my five children and see them grow and have their families.

Too many times, God had to save me and I thank him for allowing me to live to see my grandchildren. They are so funny and important to my wife and me. They have completed my life and I know they will prosper and mature into fine adults, because of their parent's upbringing.

I know several police officers that died and didn't see their children and grandchildren reach adulthood. I am so thankful that god spared my family that catastrophe.

As I was writing this book, I ask two of my granddaughters if I could include them in my book. They agreed but stated, "You have to change our names to Lucy Rosy Rainbow and Elizabeth Rainbow.

Their real names are Deja and Lael.

To all my children and grandchildren, "I love you." I have worked so hard to be there for just you.

Too Many Police Funerals
1995
Chapter 51

As I was enjoying my retirement party with all my friends, I started remembering all the police funerals that I had attended. I don't know why. I just did. I guess God wanted me to be grateful that I was still alive and I had made it, but also to remember those who hadn't. He was correct.

People were talking to me and I just couldn't hear them. I started seeing faces of police officers that had been killed in the line of duty, committed suicide, killed in car accidents, and dying while at work from heart attacks and other nature causes.

In 1972, Charlie Brown and his wife were having serious problems at home. During an argument, Officer Brown's wife threatened to leave him. The officer begged his wife not to leave, but she refused. As she was about to exit the apartment, the officer produced his service weapon, placed the barrel in his mouth, and pulled the trigger; killing himself instantly.

I remember the first female officer in Washington, DC. It was 1974. The officer was chasing a suspect who had just robbed a bank at gunpoint. The officer had stopped the suspect in a parking garage and was in the process of placing handcuffs on the suspect when he turned around and shot the officer. She died instantly.

In 1993, Officer Mike Bland, 45 years old, married with four young children, died while on duty working in the police station. He was finger printing a prisoner and just dropped dead. We attempted to revive him, but, as the doctors told us, he was dead before he hit the floor. I remembered seeing his eyes wide open looking up at me, as to say, "Kittrell, do you believe this crap? I will not see my first retirement check."

That was the kind of person Officer Bland was, always joking about everything. He was shot in the leg in 1993 as he was attempting to arrest a drug dealer. When I arrived on the scene the first thing he said to me was, "Lt. Kittrell, don't tell my wife that I was shot. She will start planning my funeral and ask how much money she will get." We just laughed as they placed him in the ambulance.

In 1992, Officer Tom Spencer; 35 years old, married with three children, died of a heart attack while he was chasing a suspect that had just burglarized someone's home. Officer Spencer was overweight and probably shouldn't have been chasing anyone.

In 1991, Sergeant Ron Wilkins was shot and killed as he and two officers attempted to arrest a man who had just assaulted his wife while inside their home. As the sergeant and officers were escorting the wife from her apartment, the husband ran after them, produced a pistol, and shot his wife and the sergeant, killing them both. The police officers shot the husband, killing him.

Officer Gloria Smith was 27 years old and a single parent with a 10 year old boy. She was young and enjoyed being a police officer. Her boyfriend shot and killed her during an argument. I was very distraught over her death. She had worked for me when she first graduated from the police academy. Another sad fact, her little boy became addicted to heroin and died of an overdose at the age of 18.

Over the next few years I became troubled and couldn't attend any more police funerals. Too many police officers died from 1972 to 1995. I dedicated this book to them for their service to the police department and the District of Columbia.

I thank God for my family and allowing me to be here and share with you my story.

Kiss your children every day and tell them how much you love them. Tomorrow is not promised.

Marco and Dorothy Kittrell